C000292451

Reginald Johnston

Chinese Mandarin

SHIONA AIRLIE

NMS Publishing Limited

Published by NMS Publishing Limited
National Museums of Scotland, Chambers Street, Edinburgh EH1 1JF

Series editor: Iseabail Macleod

ISBN 1-901663-49-3

Other titles available in the Scots' Lives series:

The Gentle Lochiel	*Miss Cranston*
Elsie Inglis	*Mungo Park*
The Scottish Suffragettes	

Forthcoming titles:

Twa Tribes
Mary Slessor

British Library Cataloguing in Publication Data
A catalogue record of this book
is available from the British Library.

Typeset in 11/13 pt Baskerville.
Internal design layout by NMS Publishing Limited.
Cover concept by Mark Blackadder. Adapted by Cara Shanley.
Cover and art section repro by Marshall Thomson Digital Communication.
Printed and bound in the United Kingdom by Bell & Bain Ltd, Glasgow.

Acknowledgements

SHIONA AIRLIE

ONE of the joys of writing about Reginald Johnston has been the opportunity it has given me, over the years, to talk to people who actually knew him. The late Mary Stewart Lockhart was the first to share her memories with me and it is she who inspired me to delve further. Mrs Sarah Markham was an equally abundant source of information and assistance.

Mrs Evelyn Battye, Mrs Irene Bell and Dr Dione Clementi are thanked for their reminiscences and help. J and R A Robertson WS, and in particular Mr Andrew Young, and their former clerk, Mr W E Hall, were of immense help in my research. The ministers in charge of St Baldred's, North Berwick and Christchurch, Edinburgh are thanked for the time they spent with me and the access they so freely gave me to church records. I am also grateful to Robert Bickers and Maxine Berg for generously sharing the fruits of their own research.

It is always a pleasure to record my gratitude to the custodians of the Stewart Lockhart Collection, the Education Board of the Merchant Company of Edinburgh, the School Governing Council of George Watson's College, and especially its Principal, Mr Frank Gerstenberg, for his continued support of the collection and all its works. Likewise, the care taken by the staff at the National Library of Scotland where the Stewart Lockhart papers are held on loan is gratefully acknowledged. Mrs Jane Cottis, the Archivist at Magdalen College, Oxford could not have been of greater assistance during my visit there and was kind enough to give me further avenues to research. The Scottish Arts Council award of a Writer's Bursary enabled me to complete my research at the Public Record Office and I am grateful for their assistance.

Finally, my thanks to Mike Gill who can probably recite this manuscript without prompting, and to Ben who may yet learn that books matter!

The illustrations in the art section of this book are credited to the following sources: *page* 1:'The Earl of Dumbarton reading a letter from the Quork.' A brush and ink drawing by Reginald Johnston (Private Collection).*page* 2The Magdalen 'Stair' in 1897 (Collection of Sarah Markham).*pages* 3-14(The Stewart Lockhart Collection with kind permission from the Education Board of the Merchant Company of Edinburgh and the School Governing Council of George Watson's College.)*page*15 (Collection of Sarah Markham).*page* 16(The Stewart Lockhart Collection – as above.)

Cover illustrations: *front* – Johnston with Chinese officials *circa* 1905; *back* – Johnston in 1927 with his Senior District Officer and staff of the Government School in Weihaiwei, holding a scroll written by Emperor Puyi; Johnston relaxes outside a temple in Beikou in Shandong Province in 1906; The seal of the Commissioner of Weihaiwei.

Places to Visit

JOHNSTON'S birthplace, Goshen Bank, is still a private house, as is his final home Eilean Righ which can be seen from the shore of the village of Ardfern in Argyll. Christchurch in Morningside and St Baldred's Church in North Berwick remain in use by the Scottish Episcopal Church. Robert Johnston's grave can be seen at Warriston Cemetery in Edinburgh. Papers from the Stewart Lockhart Collection, including more than 600 letters from Johnston, are on loan to the National Library of Scotland, while the remainder of his collection, including paintings and photographs, is lodged with George Watson's College in Edinburgh where it can be viewed by prior arrangement with the curator. Foreign and Colonial Office papers are retained at the Public Record Office in Kew. Magdalen College is open to visitors at certain times throughout the year. For those who wish to travel further afield, Weihai is well worth a visit. Now a thriving Chinese city, it is the base for the Weihai Archive Bureau which is a repository for anything to do with the city's past.

Contents

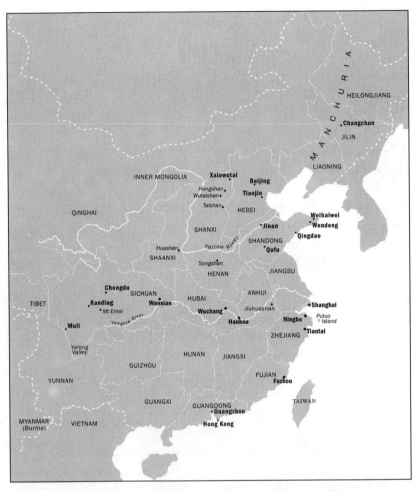

Author's Note: Johnston used the Wade-Giles system of romanisation for Chinese names. The Pinyin system is now universal, hence Peking has become Beijing; Chu-fou now Qufu. The map above, showing many of the places Reginald Johnston visited, and all Chinese names in the text, follow the Pinyin system.

*For my mother, Betty,
with love.*

Chapter 1
1874-1903

DESCRIBED in his own lifetime as eccentric, a Buddhist crank, and a recluse who was both adorable and difficult, yet wonderful with children, Reginald Johnston was indeed a strange creature; the Edinburgh lad who became a Chinese Mandarin. Perhaps the only thing his contemporaries could agree upon was that he lived an extraordinary life. This is his story.

In the nineteenth century thousands of young men just like Johnston left the mother country to work in Britain's colonies. Most of them spent unremarkable lives in remarkable places, finally meriting no more than a footnote when colonial life became history. Their work was often unremittingly boring and, perhaps because of this, many looked to other avenues to inspire their minds. Some became experts on obscure languages, others mapped unexplored regions and a number studied the culture of the societies in which they found themselves. We owe a great debt to them all. They opened up the world outside Europe to us all, and we are still learning from their studies today. They are the unsung heroes of our colonial past.

Despite their formidable achievements only a true devotee of colonial history would find their lives worth studying nowadays. In the main, theirs was a mundane existence. But a few – a very few – lived remarkable lives, and one of these was Reginald Johnston; a son of Scotland who was to make his way to the Court of the last Emperor of China. The only Scot in the Forbidden City, he was for a time at the very centre of politics in that intriguing land.

Reginald Johnston was born in Edinburgh in 1874. The second of three children, he came from a solid, middle-class family. His father, Robert, was a lawyer in the city; his mother, Isabella Irving, the daughter of an Irish minister. A year after their marriage in 1872 a daughter, Constance (Noney), was born in the family home, Goshen Bank, in the fashionable suburb of Morningside. Barely seventeen months later at 11 o'clock in the morning of 31 October 1874, their second child, Reginald Fleming Johnston, made his entrance into the world. The family was completed with the arrival of a third child, Charles Edward, two years after Reginald's birth.

Robert was a successful lawyer and a staunch member of the Conservative Club in Edinburgh. He was also closely involved in the affairs of the local Episcopal church, Christchurch. Reginald was the second child to be baptised in the newly founded church in Morningside and all three children attended church regularly. At his baptism Reginald was given the additional name, John, to follow his Christian name. It was a name he was to use sporadically throughout his life.

When it came to the question of his children's education, Robert spared no expense. Private tutors taught them the essential skills of reading and writing before they were sent off to private schools. In 1888 Reginald enrolled at Falconhall School which was situated only a few minutes walk away from their home. Founded a few years earlier, it specialised in training pupils for the competitive examinations which gained one entry into the public services and armed forces. An intelligent boy, Reginald set his sights on the Indian Civil Service which, as the premier service in the vast British Empire, was the one to which most of the brightest young men gravitated. He worked extremely hard at school and his parents encouraged him to pursue a wide range of interests. A love of music was fostered through membership of the church choir, and a fascination with history was born from visits to clan sites throughout Scotland. It should have been a happy childhood, but both Reginald and Teddy – as brother Charles preferred to be known – found life with their parents difficult. The boys cared little for their father and by the time they were adolescents family rows had become commonplace, both between Robert and his sons and Robert and his wife.

Isabella was impossible with money. Her inability to curtail spending put an increasing strain on the family's finances as time passed. Robert speculated with property to raise money and found solace in alcohol, spending hundreds of pounds with his local wine merchant. Even as a child Reginald was determined to get himself away from his 'demoralised family of drunkards and spendthrifts' as soon as he could.

He found solace from his unhappy home life by writing. He wrote wildly imaginative histories and created a series of characters which he was to keep with him for the rest of his life. These included a race called the Elephantines, of whom the drunken Earl of Dumbarton was the premier member. When Reginald eventually moved to China, the 'Earl' came with him, and established his base on the summit of Mount Everest. Unlike Johnston's father, the Earl was an amiable drunk, the life and soul of the party. Another figure he created as a child was 'The Quork'. Johnston wrote of her always carrying a 'bonnet box and green umbrella' and being notorious for creating 'scandal among all the married and unmarried men' with her outrageous behaviour. The Quork flirted with every man she met, but seems not to have been a compulsive purchaser of luxuries, so was probably not based on his mother. These strange characters belonged to Johnston's world from his youngest days and though they inhabited 'a country that had no existence except in my imagination', he was to share them with his friends and his friends' children throughout his adult life.

Despite the turbulence of home life, Reginald continued to prosper academically. In 1892, he completed his schooling but, being only seventeen, was still too young to enter the examinations for the Civil Service of India. He therefore decided to enroll at the University of Edinburgh where he quickly established himself as one of the better students in the Arts Faculty, studying English and History. Although he was a first rate student of English, it was History at which he truly excelled. In 1893 he received the prestigious Lord Rector's Prize of 25 guineas for the best essay on an historical subject. A year later he triumphed once more, this time winning the Gray Essay Prize.

Just before Reginald ended his studies at Edinburgh University, the family moved into the town centre, to Grosvenor Street in Edinburgh's West End. Part of an imposing Victorian terrace, it was a heavy, gloomy house decorated with Isabella's characteristic lavishness and in the height of the prevailing contemporary taste. Reginald loathed the place, and following the move to this house relations with his parents became so bad that neither he nor Teddy could bear to stay at home more than was absolutely necessary. Teddy was in due course to leave home for good. Reginald simply lived with family friends in Edinburgh whenever possible. Sometimes he would travel further afield, to the Highlands of Scotland. These were times when he had real fun, when he could forget his father's drunkenness and indifference and his mother's incessant spending sprees, and make full use of the opportunities presented to pursue some of his favourite pastimes; hunting, shooting and walking.

In 1894, after just two years at Edinburgh University, Reginald abandoned his studies in Scotland for a place at Magdalen College in Oxford to read Modern History. Oxford, of course, had one overriding advantage over Edinburgh as a place in which to study: it was a considerable distance from home. The move was made with few regrets and Reginald quickly fell under Magdalen's charms. Not only did he find academic stimulation there, he also gathered around him a group of friends with whom he was to remain in contact for the rest of his life.

He arrived at Magdalen on 16 October 1894 and was housed in rooms in New Building, a magnificent Georgian block inspired by Italian architecture and erected in 1733. The splendid building and its setting were quite a contrast to the sooty grime of central Edinburgh. Reginald had rooms in stair number six and on the same day as he moved into the stair, so did four other freshers: Francis Armitage, Cecil Clementi, Percy Dale and Thomas Loveday. They were to form a close and enduring friendship.

They were a bright group. Only Dale entered Magdalen as a Commoner, and all the others arrived there with scholarships. For Johnston, it was a new start. At home he was known as Reginald, or

Reggie, but his Magdalen friends were asked to call him John, and did so for the rest of his life. Other attempts at erasing the past were less successful, and before the end of the first term all the members of the stair knew of John's 'selfish and cantankerous and silent moods' which could make him 'a very difficult house-mate' at times. Despite his moods, Reginald was happy at Oxford. The college chapel was a particularly favourite place of his and he sang in the college choir. He also wrote poetry, some of which was later published.

When his mood lightened Johnston's friends found he could be charming and witty. It was not long before they were all introduced to the fantastic characters Johnston continued to create. They learned about The Quork, whom he later named Mrs Walkinshaw, and her distinctly undesirable reputation. The marvellous Earl of Dumbarton continued his wild and drunken ways and occupied himself as 'Chancellor of the Order of the Lords Elephantine'. Indeed, there were many occasions when Johnston spent more time on his poetry, music and fictional characters than he did with his studies.

At the end of his second year at Magdalen, Reginald sat the examination for entry into the Civil Service of India. In the 1890s, competitive examination was the sole means of entry into public offices and there were as many as seven candidates for every post. The highest scoring candidates were offered plum jobs in London or India and were groomed to be the future leaders of the British Empire. Additionally, there were Cadetships to the Straits Settlements, the Malay States, Ceylon and Hong Kong. All these offered a good income, a steady job and the possibility of advancement at home and abroad.

Reginald bade farewell to his college friends that summer, promising to keep in contact, but with no intention of returning to university. It must have been a considerable shock, therefore, to discover a month after the examination that he had, in his own words, 'hopelessly ploughed' paper after paper. He had little option but to return to Magdalen for a final year.

Back in Oxford once more, he continued to spend more time on non-academic work than he did studying, and was honest enough to admit to having some satisfaction when he gained a second class degree in 1898, observing that 'it was far more than I deserved; I don't suppose anyone did less work than I did'.

After graduation he returned to the oppressive atmosphere of Grosvenor Street to study for the next round of competitive exams which were to be held that August. The situation at home had not improved during his absence at Magdalen and he soon discovered that 'things at home are far too miserable to make real work possible'. Despite this, Reginald entered the examinations with a determination to pass sufficiently well to be offered a post that would take him away from home for ever. He was now almost 24, and therefore too old to qualify for entry into the Civil Service of India, but he had talked to Cecil Clementi's family, who were acquainted with Hong Kong and who had recommended the colony to him as a good posting to get, particularly because of 'the excitements that are making China interesting at present'. He therefore pinned his hopes on a sufficiently good set of marks to be offered either a Hong Kong Cadetship, or a London-based posting in the Home Civil Service.

It was a rather odd examination system in that one could attempt as many papers as one wished in a whole variety of subjects. Reginald chose eight papers covering English, French, History, Politics and Philosophy. Although his results were once again patchy (he failed French, Politics and Philosophy), he passed all the other papers and gained the second highest mark overall in the English History paper. More than 600 candidates sat the 1898 examinations, but only 98 posts were available that year. Sixty-five posts were based in India, and most of the top-scoring candidates were appointed there. Reginald, in sixty-eighth place overall, had sufficiently good marks to be selected for one of the six available posts in the Home Civil Service, but he was told that no post would be free in London until at least the spring of 1899. To wait for a London appointment meant returning home to Edinburgh for six months, the one thing he wanted to avoid. So it was that, supported by the Clementi family's suggestion, he elected to join one of the Eastern Cadetships, stating Hong Kong as his preference. It was to be a fortuitous decision.

A few more anxious weeks passed before Reginald was finally informed that he had been accepted for a Hong Kong Cadetship. Keen to leave the country as soon as possible, he was delighted when the Colonial Office gave him barely three weeks to prepare for his new life. School friends in Edinburgh held a farewell dinner for him in the city's largest hotel, the Balmoral, and even his father expressed regret at his departure, making 'a speech, which was the best I ever heard him make; but he was cut up at my going away and he showed it'. He was astonished to discover that his parents cared enough to accompany him to London to see him depart for the Far East. They would never see their son again.

Reginald set sail for Hong Kong on 17 November 1898, arriving there on Christmas Day. The journey gave him the opportunity to begin his Chinese studies and to contemplate what lay ahead for him. On arrival in Hong Kong, he knew the Government would provide him with books, teachers and living quarters. His salary would enable him to live in some comfort, being a generous $1500 HK, about £225, and this in the days when a family could live happily on £150 a year.

The Clementi family had already told Reginald of the excitements in China and Hong Kong in 1898, which was indeed a momentous year for the area. Since the 1830s most of the western powers and Japan had jostled and fought for their various toeholds within China. Mining and railway concessions brought them income and influence, and in many cities treaty ports were created. Situated on the coast and on the major rivers, these towns were the centres for western trade in China. Foreign governments were given special concessions in these areas, and Britain had representatives in most of them. China did not give these concessions willingly, but it was easy for the western powers to take advantage of her weak government for their own ends.

Throughout 1898 this scramble for concessions in China reached its height, mainly as a result of a war fought between China and Japan four years earlier. The Japanese had decimated China's forces and as a result of her victory, Japan was given territory in north China. However, the other foreign powers were not prepared to let Japan increase her influence in China without being given proportionate concessions for themselves. It was rather as if the great powers viewed China as a kind of giant cake from which everyone took a piece, the size of which depended on one's international standing. For Britain, the important thing was to retain the largest slice of the cake. Germany liked to be at least on a par with Russia, who never enjoyed seeing Japan increase her power in north China since it was too close to her own borders for comfort, and France felt the same way about Germany. China was helpless as the spoils were shared out between the powers.

Britain played little part in the negotiations with China until 1898, content to let Japan, Russia, Germany, and France do their worst before stepping in and demanding her share. In 1842 China had been forced to cede the island of Hong Kong to Britain in perpetuity, thereby enabling a British colony to be set up there. Now Britain demanded an extension to the territory in order to protect her interests in Hong Kong and was given the area known as the New Territories on a 99 year lease. She was also given a lease on land in the north of China, at a place called Weihaiwei. Neither Weihaiwei nor the New Territories were particularly large areas, both being roughly 350 square miles, but they were important to Britain. In gaining the New Territories she believed she was securing the future of Hong Kong. In gaining Weihaiwei, she hoped she was acquiring a deep-water harbour that would eventually rival those in Gibraltar and Singapore.

It was a period of deep humiliation for China and some sections of the Chinese population decided to take direct action against the rapacious foreigners. Trouble began in Shandong Province where foreign, and particularly missionary settlements, were attacked. Inflamed by a hatred of foreign, religious, and commercial encroachment within China, the attacks soon spread to other parts of the country and culminated in Peking (now Beijing) in 1900 with the siege of the foreign legations – the seat of foreign power in China – known as the Boxer Uprising. It was indeed an interesting time to arrive in the country.

The Hong Kong to which Johnston travelled was a bustling commercial centre and a mainstay of British imperial trade. In just fifty years it had been transformed from a barren landscape into a colony with impressive stone buildings in the European style. Hong Kong in the 1890s provided all the amenities a Briton abroad could wish for. There were recreational and social clubs, a dramatic society, a fine racecourse, excellent shops, churches, and a choice of impressive residences in which to live. Europeans were outnumbered by the enormous Chinese population that also lived there, but the communities were clearly segregated. The wealthiest Europeans lived on the Peak, a rocky summit which dominated Hong Kong Island and on which no Chinese were permitted to build homes. The Chinese lived on the lower parts of the island, or on the Kowloon mainland opposite the island where Britain also held a strip of territory. Chinese and non-Chinese rarely mixed after business hours.

Hong Kong might have had the appearance of a bustling British city, but this was only a veneer. British traders and officials dressed for work as they would have in the home country. Whatever the temperature, the dress code demanded dark suits and elegant cravats. Ladies, too, dressed with distinct disregard for the climate. Tight corsets and heavy gowns were *de rigeur* throughout the day. These formal European clothes contrasted starkly with the flowing, cool robes favoured by the Chinese and served to emphasise the difference between the races. In many other aspects, Hong Kong was a place with two faces. The colony had modern sanitation, but it also had annual recurrences of the plague. It contained airy, stone-built houses with verandas, but it also had horribly overcrowded slums. It was hot, humid, and smelly and no European settling there could have imagined for one minute that they were in little England, despite superficial appearances.

Johnston was met on arrival by the Acting Colonial Secretary, Mr Sercombe Smith, who whisked him off to his house to share in the family Christmas dinner. He then had a few days to recover from his sea journey and find his way around the place before any real work started. Reginald wasted no time in plunging himself into the whirl of

Hong Kong society. Within two days of his arrival he had become a member of the colony's premier club, the Hong Kong Club, and introductions to other members ensured that he was most hospitably treated until the time came for him to begin his Chinese studies.

From the moment he set foot in Hong Kong, Johnston's spirits lightened. The heat and the dirt did not bother him one bit and it was a place he immediately took to, comparing the scenery to that of 'a miniature Scotch Highlands'. The landscape on the Chinese mainland did indeed look at that time very similar to parts of Scotland. Rolling, low hills swept into the Kowloon peninsula from the colony. Covered in lush growth with small trees and shrubs one can understand how this landscape held a certain familiarity for the Scots who saw it. Of course, Hong Kong had one thing never found in Scotland: warm rain.

After a week or so enjoying Hong Kong's pleasures, it was time for Johnston to travel to the mainland city of Guangzhou, as Canton is now known, to learn Chinese. The unrest which had been brewing in China for some months had by that time spread to the south of the country, but despite the unsettled situation the Government still deemed it safe enough to send the colony's newest Cadets to Guangzhou. As this city was only about 80 miles to the north of Hong Kong, the authorities probably felt that the Cadets would not be too far away from the colony to escape back there quickly if the need arose.

If Hong Kong was hot and dirty, Guangzhou was even more so. Although there was a foreign community there, they lived in their own quarter, and the rest of the city was entirely Chinese in character. Johnston would have been given a flavour of China in Hong Kong, but nothing can have prepared him for the noise and crowds of Guangzhou. Only three months after he left Scotland he was thrust into a completely alien environment and he loved it.

His new accommodation must have helped. The Yamen (the official residence in which he stayed) was the British Consul's house, which he shared with several other Cadets who had been posted into service in the East. It was a spacious house and in addition to a fine garden had its own Deer Park, so the Cadets lived in some luxury. Cooks, coolies, valets, and a gardener ensured that their every need was catered for. After three months in Guangzhou, Johnston found time to write to his friend from Magdalen, Loveday, enthusing about his new life:

China and the Chinese are intensely interesting, not only on account of the present tottering condition of China. The Chinese language is hard, especially the written language, but I think its difficulties have been much over-rated. I can easily make myself understood among people already ... I work just when and how I like. There are four of us cadets (2 belonging to the Malay States and 2 of us Hongkong men) living at this Yamen. Each of us has a Chinese teacher of his own. I make mine come at 10 each morning and he goes away at lunchtime. At 2 he returns (if I feel inclined to work in the afternoon) and stays till about 3.30. My time is absolutely at my own disposal and I can take a holiday when I like; the only stipulation being that I pass periodical exams (about 3 in number), held at Hongkong. The minimum amount of work required for them is very small .... Life is a most luxurious affair. My boy brings me tea and toast every morning in bed at 7, we have a fat breakfast of 3 or 4 courses ... at 9, an excellent lunch ... and dinner at 7.30 p.m. which would put the Magdalen hall to shame .... We drink wine every day, sometimes a good deal. And with all of this, I am saving money .... Englishmen in China evidently live a devil of a fast life, both as regards wine and women.

The Cadets certainly managed to make the most of the social opportunities offered to them there. Wise Chinese merchants, fully aware that one day the Cadets could well become their administrative masters, offered them hospitality. One of the more unusual evenings spent by Reginald in the company of such a merchant was a visit to a 'flower boat' – the polite name for a floating brothel. Not surprisingly, Reginald was captivated by the atmosphere of the boat. Even the musicians were prostitutes and they looked after Johnston as they were expected to, so that 'at times during the evening I had two girls on my knees at the same time'. The dinner was in the Chinese style, several courses long, and Johnston used chopsticks for the first time. When the musicians were not petting him they provided a musical accompani-

17

ment during the meal. In later years Johnston was to learn to enjoy the strange cadences of Chinese music. He found the music that night a 'bewildering thing'; nevertheless he decided on the spot to make 'a sort of hobby of it' thereafter. By the end of the evening he formed a firm opinion about the Chinese: 'I get on jolly well with the Chinamen I have come across. I like them.' His love affair with China had begun.

Cadets normally spent two years in Guangzhou before sitting their final exams, becoming Passed Cadets, and assuming office within the government of Hong Kong. No such luxury was to be afforded to Johnston, however, and after only seven months of language training he was brought back to Hong Kong in the summer of 1899 to provide cover for officers on leave of absence. His first job, fortunately, required no proficiency in the Chinese language.

In 1898, a new Governor had arrived in Hong Kong. Sir Henry Blake, a rather genial figure, arrived during the preparations to lease the New Territories from China. By 1899, when Johnston was recalled from Guangzhou, the process of leasing the area was well under way. James Stewart Lockhart, the Colony's Colonial Secretary, oversaw the organisation of the lease and set up the British administration there. Everything, from a geographical and economic survey of the territory to population censuses and decisions about its administration, had to be done from scratch and it all required Stewart Lockhart's attention. His presence in the New Territories meant that to all intents and purposes Hong Kong was without the services of a Colonial Secretary, traditionally the person most essential to the administration of a colony. Stewart Lockhart was one of Hong Kong's longest-serving officers, having arrived from Scotland as a Cadet more than 20 years earlier. His absence from the centre of government in order to supervise the newly leased territory put an unbearable strain on the administration, so Johnston was brought to Hong Kong to assist in whatever way he could.

Two councils assisted Governor Blake, and it was a Clerk of Councils' duty to attend all meetings and minute the proceedings. This was the post now allotted to Johnston. Attendance as Clerk in both councils gave him a marvellous opportunity to study the workings of colonial government, even if most of his time was spent writing agendas and taking minutes of the meetings. He found the meetings of the Executive Council particularly interesting 'as all the secrets of the colony are discussed there'. Certainly, he enjoyed his first taste of administrative work and impressed the Governor with his industry.

But within a matter of weeks Johnston was taken away from the council chamber and sent to the New Territories to help with land registration. Every inch of land had to be surveyed for the Government mapping service. The Government then had to be certain exactly who owned which pieces of land. The population was, in the main, peasant farmers. Some families had lived in the same villages for hundreds of years, subdividing the land into ever-smaller parcels as their households expanded. Hong Kong was a prosperous colony with high property values. The New Territories were primarily farmland and countryside with little commercial value. However, the moment the territory was leased to Britain, land speculation began. Everyone was aware that the value of the farmland would rise enormously in the years to come and there was suddenly a clamour for property rights. Before many months had passed, a number of villagers were producing forged documents to prove land ownership. The problem was complicated further because some people with forged documents had actually been farming the land they purported to own for generations. The mess was to take years to resolve and in 1899 took up huge amounts of the administration's time.

For two months Johnston worked in oppressive heat and humidity without complaint. Some days he would be assisting the Government surveyors to plot the newly acquired area. On other days he would be seated under a flimsy bamboo shade trying to decipher scraps of paper with land claims written on them, deciding not only what land was referred to in the documents but whether or not the claim was a genuine one. It was hard work, and must have challenged his newly acquired knowledge of Chinese to the utmost. To his credit, Johnston stuck to the task with dogged determination.

Within a few weeks Johnston had impressed his superiors to such an extent that when the next staff crisis came, Blake and Stewart Lockhart had no hesitation in giving him the work:

> *I was telephoned for by Lockhart, and summoned to go back to Hong Kong with bag, baggage and boy. When I got there I discovered that Buckle, the Assistant Colonial Secretary ... had resigned the service and was on the point of leaving ... I was chosen to fill the post in an 'acting' capacity .... My cadet's pay was at once more than doubled, and I am afraid my success caused some annoyance to the 3 cadets who are senior to me.*

The Assistant Colonial Secretary's job was a demanding one, and even Johnston had to admit that 'my work is hard'. He had lived in the East for less than a year, and suddenly he was presented with a job which involved working in the upper levels of the administration. Papers had to be drafted for council meetings, ordinances prepared, the raft of paperwork from the Colonial Office read, digested, actioned, and passed on to the appropriate official. It was an appointment normally only given to Passed Cadets with a year or two of service and Johnston's friend, Cecil Clementi, correctly observed this to be 'a most exceptional appointment for a probationer'.

The work brought Johnston under Stewart Lockhart's direct control and the two men soon became closely acquainted. Reginald learned to admire the Colonial Secretary's administrative ability and grasp of the colony's affairs, while Stewart Lockhart appreciated Johnston's quirky sense of humour and able mind. In many ways he must have seen in Johnston a mirror of himself as a young man in Hong Kong, and Stewart Lockhart began to encourage his Cadet to broaden his horizons as his own had been two decades earlier. The Colonial Secretary was a sinophile of no small repute and he began to encourage Johnston to extend his Chinese studies beyond the language into other areas such as history and philosophy, believing that to appreciate China fully one had to understand the culture and society, not simply know the language. Despite the difference in their ages, the two colonial officials soon became firm friends, sharing a love of Chinese culture that was to endure until the end of their lives.

The year 1899 not only brought Johnston recognition of his abilities but also the welcome tidings that Clementi was to join him in Hong Kong. Initially, Johnston and Clementi had little opportunity to spend time together. Clementi started his language training in Guangzhou while Johnston was fully occupied with work in the New Territories. Clementi's time in Guangzhou was to be as short lived as Johnston's had been. Unrest was now so prevalent in the south that in July 1900 the government in Hong Kong was forced to withdraw all its Cadets from Guangzhou. Clementi immediately moved into a house which Johnston had acquired on the Hong Kong mainland in Kowloon, and looked forward to reviving the friendship they had started at Magdalen.

The warmth of the friendship was still there, but Clementi had forgotten about Johnston's black moods and eccentric ways. After only four months in Johnston's company he 'decided that at all costs I must take a house and live by myself .... Out here I have decided that he [Johnston] is impossible. He retains all his Oxford faults .... He is unable to work: he is unable to carry on a serious conversation'. Despite these irritations, Clementi was extremely fond of Johnston and did not want to cause his friend anguish by leaving the house abruptly. Johnston, after all, had given Clementi rooms in his home at short notice in an act of friendship and to leave because of his host's habits, however irritating, might appear churlish. Clementi was working like a man possessed, determined to pass his Cadet exams in record time. He was growing up; Johnston had, in many ways, yet to do so. Face was saved all round when Johnston was promoted to be the Governor's Private Secretary. This entailed a move to Government House for Johnston, and an equally swift promotion for Clementi who took over his friend's post as Acting Assistant Colonial Secretary and Clerk of Councils.

Staff shortages a few months later would force a further move upon Clementi and return Johnston to all three posts in 1901: Private Secretary to the Governor, Acting Assistant Colonial Secretary and

Clerk of Councils. Despite this quite intolerable workload, he took Clementi's criticisms to heart and buckled down to work, passing his final Cadet examinations later that year. This was no small achievement, for the examinations were rigorous. They included having a conversation with a Chinese who spoke no English and translating cases drawn from Government files from Chinese into English and from English into Chinese. Fortunately, his work in the New Territories had given him plenty of practical experience in this area.

In July 1902, Johnston's father died. Johnston was due leave from the service that year, and Blake was a Governor of sufficient compassion to have ensured that, should his Private Secretary wish it, he would be given the necessary time to make the journey back to Scotland to settle his father's estate. However, Reginald made the apparently astonishing decision not to go home but instead to spend his leave travelling through Yunnan in south-west China and Tongking (in present-day Vietnam) to the Shan States in Burma (present-day Myanmar) and Bangkok. It was a journey that was to keep him away from Hong Kong until 1903.

While Reginald made his escape into the wilderness on the edges of China, his father was being buried with all the pomp and ceremony befitting his status. A funeral service in the Episcopal cathedral of St Mary's in Edinburgh was followed by an interment in the family grave at Warriston Cemetery, a fine Victorian necropolis in the city. The obituary in the local newspaper, *The Scotsman*, recorded how Robert's 'hosts of friends ... are eminently poorer to-day by his unexpected removal'. Many of them were indeed to be the poorer for his passing, for within a few weeks of his sudden death from pneumonia it became clear that he had never been the respectable Edinburgh lawyer which outward appearances had suggested. Robert Johnston died leaving an estate so debt-ridden that Isabella was left with only one course of action: to declare her deceased husband bankrupt.

Before long, everyone in Edinburgh knew that, in the words of the estate's judicial factor, Henry Shiells, 'Mr Johnston from the beginning seems to have made no distinction ... between his own money and his clients' money'. Robert Johnston died owing almost £29,000. He had built up a minor property empire within the city but unfortunately had used his clients' money to pay for the properties he purchased. It was not only his clients who were to suffer financial losses; the lists of creditors to his estate included wine merchants, coal merchants, butchers, ironmongers, clothiers, stationers, opticians, bakers, and laundry-men. The debts were so great that even when all of Robert's assets were realised, the people who had so unwisely given him credit were repaid at a rate of only one shilling and eleven pence to the pound: a tenth of the value of the debt.

Isabella and her children faced public disgrace, for bankruptcy carried a huge social stigma. She was forced to move from the family home and to watch as treasured possessions including pictures, books, and family silver were sold by public auction. To add to her and her children's humiliation, the family's possessions were advertised in the local press prior to the auction. A household sale of furniture included the Johnstons' 'carved oak sideboard, dining table ... mahogany book-cases, Broadwood piano, walnut writing tables ... clocks, bronzes, Dresden china dessert service, beds and bedding, washstands, gong and ... bagatelle table'. Isabella remained strangely detached from the proceedings, despite the terrible disgrace of it all. It is some measure of the woman and her attitude to money that, fully aware of the impending legal action over her husband's affairs, she still managed to spend three guineas – a sum greater than the average weekly wage of the day – on a hat for the funeral. She, it would seem, was as much to blame for Robert's financially parlous state as was he.

Under the circumstances, it was perhaps not surprising that Reginald decided to hide himself in deepest China rather than face the disgrace of his father's legacy. Certainly, the whole affair wounded him deeply, and he vowed he would 'never again set foot in Scotland unless I could do so as a free man – with all my father's liabilities paid off in full'. Thereafter no mention would be made, even to his closest friends, about his parents or his family. Indeed, in later life, most people who knew him, including distant relations, assumed he was an only child.

Not even Clementi was told of the situation, though he was sufficiently close to Johnston to realise that something was wrong, and to voice his worries about his friend's increasingly eccentric and moody behaviour to Loveday.

Despite his feelings about his family, Johnston did not abandon them entirely. He knew as well as anyone of his mother's ability to dispose of money, but even so he sent the family lawyers, J and R A Robertson, £350 to enable her to set up home in rented accommodation. It was all the money he had; every penny he had saved since his arrival in Hong Kong. The extent of his financial sacrifice should not be underestimated, for it left him without any financial cushion whatsoever. Isabella would never again be able to consider herself wealthy, but she continued to spend money she did not possess until her dying day.

Whereas Reginald's career did not suffer from his father's misdemeanours (though this situation might well have been different had the story become common knowledge in Hong Kong), it was Teddy who fared worst from the sorry affair. In 1899 he had moved to the small town of North Berwick, a fashionable summer resort not far down the coast from Edinburgh. There he became organist and choirmaster at St Baldred's, the main Episcopal church in the town. Teddy was well liked and successful in his work, and was described by the vestry committee as being both talented and hard working. But this ability was not to save him when the truth about his father's affairs became public, and he was forced to leave his post. A respectable congregation such as St Baldred's simply could not afford to have as their choirmaster a man from a bankrupt family. Just like Reginald, Teddy felt the humiliation of the situation was too much to bear and he fled the country, leaving Scotland for ever to move to America where he sheltered in the anonymity of New York.

At the same time as Teddy was being asked to leave St Baldred's, Reginald was recovering from his family's shame on a journey through the west of China and thence across Vietnam and into Laos where he sailed down the Nam-Ou River in a canoe. An anonymous Cadet whom he never mentions in his later notes about their travels, and whom he seems to have rather ignored, joined him on the journey. They reached the border of China and Vietnam without incident and then made the extraordinary decision to dismiss their interpreter. The first anyone in Hong Kong knew about the situation was when the 'interpreter suddenly returned with 15 cases of luggage' and a note from Johnston to Clementi saying that 'owing to the delay he was sending away all his impedimenta including food and blankets and pushing on with no more than they could carry if necessary on their backs'. Clementi was understandably alarmed that Johnston had 'vindicated his reputation for eccentricity', without understanding why his friend was behaving this way.

Despite Clementi's belief that 'such a performance is most foolhardy and even if John comes through it without serious illness he will have suffered privations so severe that his holiday trip can scarcely have been one of enjoyment', Johnston continued on his way. This was not a holiday for him, but a way of erasing the deep shock of the events surrounding his father's death. Having divested himself of his belongings he travelled through Vietnam and Laos with two Chinese coolies and even they deserted him during his canoe trip. Their desertion taught him a lesson, which was all the more poignant with the knowledge of his family's acquisitive instincts. He later related with some pride how he abandoned all his luggage, keeping only what he could carry in his hands and pockets. This method of travelling obviously had a profound effect upon him and he later wrote in his book *From Peking to Mandalay* that 'it was then that my eyes were first opened to the fact that civilised man encumbers himself with a great many material possessions which he could quite well do without'. Johnston could not avoid or ignore his family's misfortunes entirely, but the journey helped heal some wounds and also marked a crucial point in his life. The gentle Lao-Shans showed him how Buddhism could become a way to cope with life and it would seem that this was when he began to adopt the Buddhist philosophy for himself. He was to continue to study the Buddhist canon for the rest of his life, more as an intellectual pursuit than as a religion, but in 1903 it was probably the one thing that kept him sane as his family world crumbled before him.

In January 1903, Reginald returned to his work in Hong Kong. Although Stewart Lockhart had now left the colony, Johnston still had plenty of close companions including other Cadets, colleagues, and Clementi, who shared a houseboat with him for a while. Despite his easy-going social lifestyle, Johnston was extremely unhappy. His father's disgrace, and the threat that it might become public knowledge in Hong Kong, hung like a sword over his head. Aware of what had happened to his brother, he must have been terrified that the same thing would happen to him.

Johnston was a sociable man. Many who knew him recalled what a pleasant companion he could be, and there were few women who were not entranced by him. Of moderate stature with fair hair and blue eyes, he could be counted attractive, but it was his witty company that most would later recall. Yet he also had a deep need to spend time on his own. The 1902 journey showed him the benefits of such a life and it also whetted his desire to explore China further and to get to know and understand more of her customs and people. Hong Kong offered no opportunities in this area, and the colony also held the additional risk that someone from her large Scottish community might hear of his family's sad situation. It was obvious to Johnston that he would have to leave Hong Kong if he were to feel any peace in himself. A year later he was granted his wish.

Chapter 2
1904-1918

THE territory which took Johnston away from Hong Kong was Weihaiwei, the area leased from China at the same time as the New Territories, in 1898. Situated in Shandong Province in the northeast of China, it was important for its sheltered, deep-water harbour which provided an excellent base for the British navy. In 1901 the British Government decided that Weihaiwei should be run by a civil administrator, and James Stewart Lockhart was appointed Commissioner.

Weihaiwei was a far smaller administration than that of Hong Kong, with a single deputy to assist the Commissioner. From the outset, Stewart Lockhart was determined to bring Johnston up to be that assistant. However, the Colonial Office selected Robert Walter, a Passed Cadet with two years' more service than Johnston, as the Commissioner's first deputy. Although Walter and Stewart Lockhart had an amicable working relationship, they were never truly close and Stewart Lockhart continued to harbour hopes of bringing Johnston to the territory. His opportunity came when Walter announced in 1903 that he was to take leave in Britain the following year. Stewart Lockhart immediately wrote to the Colonial Office asking that Johnston replace Walter. On 21 April 1904 Johnston was appointed as Walter's temporary replacement. He arrived in Weihaiwei two weeks later amidst much celebration at Government House.

China has a written language which is common to the entire country. However, each region uses its own dialect of this language and these dialects vary so much from one region to the next that a speaker from Shandong, for example, cannot understand a speaker from south China unless they have learned each other's dialect. It is some measure of Stewart Lockhart's keenness to have Johnston in Weihaiwei that he appointed him even though Johnston, at that point fluent in Cantonese, spoke only a smattering of Mandarin, and knew nothing of the local dialect.

Weihaiwei was a fashionable holiday resort for those who wished to avoid the oppressive heat and humidity of Hong Kong. It was also the summer base for the British China Squadron. Thus, there was no shortage of interesting and varied company during those months. In winter, however, it became a place of solitude, isolation and bitter cold. The navy moved to the warmer waters of the south and few visitors arrived. With the European population reduced to a handful of souls, one was forced to make one's own amusements. Johnston would have noticed many differences between Hong Kong and Weihaiwei. The territory had no electricity or telephones. There were no proper roads to speak of. Sanitation was rudimentary and coolies collected the night soil from homes each morning in order to fertilise the fields. There was only one hotel and a school, and no grand clubs in which to enjoy a drink with other gentlemen in the evening. Although Weihaiwei was completely without the bustle and buzz of Hong Kong and it lacked crowds and grand buildings, it did have its own advantages. It had a generally pleasant climate and was relatively free from disease, despite the lack of modern sanitation. The Chinese population, which numbered about 150,000 people, were in the main farmers. There was little poverty or deprivation in the territory and unlike Hong Kong there were no slums and virtually no crime.

Although Weihaiwei was of a size similar to that of Hong Kong's New Territories, in appearance it was quite different. Liugong Island, with its deep-water harbour, provided a focal point from the shore of the capital, Port Edward. The capital itself was a small settlement in which most of the territory's European residents lived. Government House, a modest single-storey building, was built there, as were the government offices. A small pier on the shoreline provided anchorage for the launches that plied between Port Edward and the island each day in summer. Weihaiwei's mainland was bounded by several miles of gentle coastline, with sheltered bays and sandy beaches and a series of low hills extended from this coast into Shandong Province.

Weihaiwei lacked any really stunning scenery. The inhabitants of her 300 villages and hamlets had long ago cut down for fuel what trees had once existed and when Johnston arrived the land was covered sparsely with scrub oak and rough grass on uncultivated hills. Between these low hills, flat plains were covered in a bold pattern of fields. A network of streams ensured that drought was a rare occurrence and the only other features in this rural backwater were the myriad dirt tracks which served instead of roads. The contrast to Hong Kong was enormous.

After only three months in Weihaiwei, Stewart Lockhart sent Johnston out of the territory on a government assignment. In 1903 the Commissioner had travelled into China to make a pilgrimage to Qufu, in Shandong Province, where Confucius had been born. There he met Confucius' direct descendant, Duke Kong, and during the course of that visit he promised to send the Duke a portrait of the British king, Edward VII, on his return to Weihaiwei. The portrait took longer than anticipated to organise, and it was not ready for almost a year. But the wait until the summer of 1904 was worthwhile, for the large photo-graph arrived in Weihaiwei resplendent in a magnificent carved gilt frame housed in an equally magnificent carved box impressed with the royal monogram. It was Johnston's task to deliver this to the Duke.

Reginald was as resplendent as the magnificent portrait when he set out on his journey. Dressed in top hat and frock coat, he must have looked extremely out of place in the Chinese countryside through which he escorted the photograph which was carried in its own sedan chair. Reginald left Weihaiwei on 15 August for the first part of his journey to the regional capital, Jinan. A steamer took him down the coast to the German-run treaty port of Qingdao, just an overnight's sail from Weihaiwei. There he boarded the train for the 14-hour journey to Jinan on the railway which had been opened that spring. Although travelling by train saved Johnston from what would have been an other-wise dirty and bumpy journey over Shandong's primitive roadways, it was hardly in itself a trip of great comfort. He was later to report that the 'rate of progress is not rapid, and the great number of stoppages tends to make the journey somewhat monotonous', as indeed it was, covering 260 miles at less than 19 miles an hour. Still, it was better than any of the other alternatives.

Whereas his journey to date had been quite pleasant, the next stage was to be less so. In winter the roads of Shandong were dust bowls, but the rains came in summer and reduced them to muddy torrents: 'The surface of the roads, moreover, was at all times and in all places so broken and ragged that the most stoutly-built cart ever seen on an English country lane would have been speedily wrenched and jerked into a bundle of firewood.' It was to take Johnston four days of hard travelling to cover the 120 miles from Jinan to Qufu. The only salvation was the hospitality offered each day by local magistrates on the instruction of the Governor: 'Every inn at which we stopped ... was carefully swept and garnished ... and scarlet draperies hung outside the main door of the inn and in the courtyard.' As a result of this attention, Johnston found that at every stop there was 'an eager and expectant crowd waiting to catch sight of the strange foreign monster'. He seems to have rather enjoyed his unexpected notoriety.

The approach to the ancient walled city of Qufu was an impressive sight and well worth the uncomfortable journey there. Situated on a plain, the walls were visible from miles away. Johnston arrived in style. As he entered through the city gates he was met by a number of Duke Kong's own attendants 'clad in one of the handsomest uniforms I have seen in China: composed of black, red and yellow stripes so arranged as to represent a tiger's skin'. With this colourful escort, he made his way into the city.

Aged 33, only slightly older than Johnston, Duke Kong was guardian of his ancestral temples. Because of his elevated position, he could not leave Qufu without the express permission of the Emperor and therefore welcomed Johnston's visit as a pleasant diversion. The Duke gave Johnston a tour of his magnificent estate, an enormous complex that covered several hundred acres. As well as the family mansion there were temples, halls, pavilions and parkland. The burial ground of his famous ancestor alone covered 50 acres and was once the largest park in China. This was a place of startling beauty and extraordinary contrasts. Only a simple stone slab commemorated the birthplace of Confucius and yet the temple, which was built in celebration of him, comprised almost 500 rooms.

On the second day of Johnston's visit, Edward VII's portrait was processed through the city's streets in front of large crowds. Johnston followed behind in a scarlet sedan chair and he and the portrait were greeted at the gates of the palace with an artillery salute. Having finally handed over the gift, he had another pleasant meeting with the Duke before returning to an inn for the evening. On the next, his final, day in Qufu, Johnston was invited to dinner by the Duke. This was a rare treat, for the Duke's kitchens were famous for their food. It was a splendid end to a splendid visit, and Johnston relished the excellent feast which included 'the inevitable bird's nest and shark's fin as well as copious quantities of wine'. It was a fitting end to an extraordinary piece of government duty.

He left Qufu the next morning, but the fun was not completely over. On his return journey to Jinan, he altered his route in order to visit one of the sacred mountains of China, Taishan. There are several holy mountains in China and Johnston was eventually to visit them all. The reasons for their sanctity probably date back to prehistory, and they were later adopted by various Chinese religions as places of particular importance. Taishan, perhaps because of its relative proximity to Beijing and its devotion to the cult of the emperor, was generally rated to be the most famous of the sacred hills, and so it is not surprising that Johnston wanted to go and visit it.

The sacred mountains generally have well-paved pathways leading to their summits. Taishan, 5500 feet high, is ascended by climbing up a series of broad stone stairways. These are dotted with temple complexes, shrines, and stone inscriptions all the way up. Johnston was particularly intrigued by the fact that wealthy pilgrims hired workmen to carve inscriptions in inaccessible places on the mountain as a sign of their wealth and devotion. At the summit a temple was prepared for Johnston to stay in for the night so that he could experience one of the especial beauties of the mountain the next morning: the sunrise. It was one of the highlights of the visit.

Once back in Weihaiwei, most of his time was taken up with court work. The laws of the territory were based on British law, although Chinese customs were adhered to whenever possible. In Imperial China an area the size of Weihaiwei would have been administered by a local official, appointed by the Provincial Governor. This magistrate would be responsible not only for collecting taxes but also for the maintenance of law and order. Because of the general inefficiency and corruption of the Chinese system taxes were high, and in local disputes the magistrate levied a charge for settling disagreements. Under British rule, Weihaiwei's population discovered two immediate advantages over rule by their own officials: taxes were lower and litigation was free. Thus an enormous part of Johnston's daily work involved settling disputes among Weihaiwei's Chinese residents. These were commonly about land or matrimonial conflicts; very much the stuff of everyday peasant life. Reginald undoubtedly found it infuriating at times to have to suffer the daily minutiae of the petty disagreements presented to him. Even so, he always looked upon his post as magistrate as one of high responsibility.

His work as a magistrate did not have an auspicious start. One of his first acts was to rid his court of its Chinese interpreter who had been taking bribes. Thereafter, he heard with monotonous regularity one civil case after another. In his first year alone, he heard more than 400 cases and read more than 1000 petitions. Court cases followed a predetermined pattern. The plaintiff would employ a professional petition writer to set out the case, which Johnston would then read. A date would be set for a hearing, summonses sent out, and the case heard on the due date. Judicial decorum had to be observed at all times, though the process was often hampered by both plaintiff and defendant bringing large numbers of people to court to testify to their good character. Sometimes the proprieties of court were not observed, despite Reginald's best efforts. On one occasion he decided against the defendant in a debt case, whereupon the man asked to be executed instantly. Johnston, not unnaturally, refused the request and the man was then 'carried out screaming, and attracted some languid attention in the street by inviting my tingzhais [attendants] to remove his head in the public thoroughfare'. Apart from these moments of high drama, the courtroom served one immensely useful function for Johnston. The daily round of cases gave him total fluency in the local dialect before he had completed his first year in the territory.

When it became clear, in October 1905, that Walter was to return permanently to Weihaiwei, Johnston applied for leave. He had decided not to return to Hong Kong and was prepared to resign following his leave rather than do so. He made his views clear to the Commissioner before he left on leave, and also wrote to the Colonial Office to tell them that he 'wished to be transferred from Hong Kong to some congenial post elsewhere, where I should be allowed some personal initiative and independence of activity and be brought into intimate connection with native races'. Stewart Lockhart supported his request, asking that Johnston be stationed permanently in Weihaiwei, citing his excellent work in the territory: 'He gained the confidence of the Chinese: is able to speak the local dialect; and I am sure the Chinese inhabitants of this Territory would welcome his return.' The officials in London took quite a different view of Johnston, citing 'his extravagant views as to his own position and importance' as a good reason not to give him a new appointment.

Johnston's absence gave Stewart Lockhart the opportunity to plan the administration of the territory in such a way as to create a permanent post for him there, whatever the views of the Colonial Office on this matter. He proposed to split Weihaiwei into two administrative divisions, north and south. A Secretary to Government would be responsible for the north division and would be based in Port Edward, while a District Officer would be responsible for the south division and live in the southern countryside. The new District Officer post was tailor-made for Johnston. It would give him the opportunity to work in isolation among the Chinese, precisely the type of posting he desired. In February 1906 the Commissioner was told that he was to have his wish, but it was several months more before Johnston heard the glad news for he was on his next great adventure; an overland journey across China to Tibet and down to Burma.

Johnston took his little bull terrier, Jim, with him on the adventure. Jim must have been an exceedingly fit small dog, for he accompanied his master for the whole of the journey. Johnston's human company was comprised in the main of boys employed for a stage or so as guides or baggage handlers. The remainder of his party, in addition to his personal servant-cum-interpreter, were Chinese soldiers. The Chinese Government insisted upon their presence for any foreigner travelling through China. They, like the coolies, only travelled part of the route, changing over with a new team at appropriate stages. Johnston was hardly travelling in solitary splendour, but he did make his journey with a far smaller team than most contemporary travellers.

He began by travelling north-west from Weihaiwei to make a visit to Beijing to collect the necessary papers and permissions from the British Legation there. He then travelled south to Hankou where a month-long boat trip up the Yangtze River took him deep into western China. On the way he stopped at some of the treaty ports. For any traveller, even one as intrepid as Johnston, the British consular network in these ports was a lifeline. Their offices could cash cheques and exchange money for him, act as a postal address to which letters could be forwarded, and even, on occasion, offer a bit of civilised company. It was for this reason that Johnston, even when he was travelling in the most remote parts of China, would make sometimes lengthy detours to find a city where the British had a treaty with the Chinese which enabled them to trade and where they would therefore have a consular presence. For the consuls themselves, a visit from a fellow official was always a welcome break from the solitude and hardship of life in a remote Chinese city.

He left the Yangtze at the Chinese trading centre of Wanxian in Sichuan Province. An enormous province, the size of France, large parts of it were quite unknown to Europeans at that time. Johnston was already far from the reaches of the main British treaty areas and so stayed in an establishment which tended to be the other port of call for European travellers, the local mission. He stayed with the missionaries for one night, admitting that 'I have not told them I am a Buddhist!' while he enjoyed their quarters.

For almost two months Johnston roamed across the vast province, eventually reaching a sacred mountain, Mount Emei. *En route* he stopped to explore some prehistoric dwellings 'and a Buddhist monastery of exceptional interest' where he joined a band of Tibetan pilgrims. Quite what they thought of their strange travelling companion and his dog is not known, but Johnston did note 'Jim is still alive, as many Chinese monks know to their cost .... He walked or ran the whole way from Wanxian to Chengdu, an overland journey of 14 days, doing his 25 or 30 miles a day without turning a hair. He is now to make the ascent of Mount Emei. Fortunately he is in blissful ignorance of the fact'. The mountain was 11,000 feet high, but Jim – and Johnston – managed the ascent without any problems, even though it was very early in the season and the snow-line came down about 5000 or 6000 feet below the summit. He made the most of his visit, exploring many of the 20 or so temples there dedicated to the Buddhist god of pervading goodness whose abode is said to be on the mountain. These, and the spectacular views he encountered, also served to increase his interest in the wonderful holy hills.

For the next few weeks he travelled slowly north and west on one of the most exhilarating parts of his adventure. Crossing mountain passes 10,000 feet above sea level, and travelling 'through gorgeous scenery', he reached Kanding in early April. Although in Sichuan, Kanding was quite Tibetan in character. When he arrived at the town, which is 9000 feet above sea level, it was still snowbound. The bustling little centre on the main tea-trading route from Beijing to Lhasa captivated Johnston, although it was a huge disappointment to arrive there and discover that conflict between the Tibetans and the Chinese meant that he would not be permitted to enter Tibet proper. He therefore decided to travel to Yunnan, staying first in Kanding for three weeks to enable him to learn some Tibetan. There was a degree of logic in this. To go south to Yunnan he would have to travel through country which, although geographically Chinese, was entirely Tibetan in every other sense. A smattering of the local language would therefore be helpful.

His route to Yunnan Province was to take him through the Yalong Valley, one of the least explored regions of China. Even today no roads transverse large parts of the area, which is inhospitable, mountainous, and very sparsely populated. This was to be a real challenge and by mid April he was ready to undertake this, the most taxing, part of his journey. The first stage took 40 days and was not without risk. In addition to the threat of robbers, ruling lamas were at war with one another as well as with the Chinese. Also, the geography of the area made it a difficult route to follow, with high, snow-covered passes and unbridged rivers. In the knowledge that he was going to be crossing extremely inhospitable terrain with little opportunity to add to his supplies of food, Johnston further prepared himself before leaving Kanding by mastering the art of surviving on the staple Tibetan fare of *tsamba*, a fairly unappetising mixture of tea, barley meal and yak butter.

The trek was a real adventure and even Johnston admitted to having a 'very rough time of it'. Some of the mountain passes were over 17,000 feet high, and on one of the highest the snow was so deep that his mules had trouble walking and one died. For almost a month he saw few signs of human habitation and the people he did see were 'entirely Tibetan in race, language, custom and everything else', so he was grateful for the rudimentary language lessons he had taken in Kanding. His acquaintance with tsamba also stood him in good stead, for it was all he and his small party ate for most of the journey. Occasionally, he would manage to find and shoot the odd pheasant to relieve their diet, and a few other times he bought a goat from local people. Wearing furs and sheepskin boots, and with smoked glasses to protect against sun blindness, the difficulties he encountered *en route* were considerable. Yet, despite the steep climbs, high winds, snowstorms and oxygen deprivation, his party achieved an astonishing ten or twelve miles each day. One of the most frightening parts of the journey came when he had to cross the Yalong River. The 'bridge' was a single bamboo rope with a pulley mechanism, slung 120 feet above the fast-flowing river. His description in *From Peking to Mandalay* of getting across on it is quite hair-raising: 'The weight of our bodies only took us about two-thirds of the total distance, and from that point we had to proceed by throwing our legs over the rope and pulling ourselves upwards, inch by inch, hand over hand.' This episode under-lines his extraordinary physical fitness; a fact he tends to play down. The mountain crossings alone would have defeated most men, but the crossing of the Yalong was an experience only the toughest explorer could have contemplated.

The final trek into Muli, the first town he had seen since leaving Kanding, was not much better, although the mountains were not so high as the ones they had previously crossed. Johnston slept on the snow each night with only a blanket to protect him, a form of camp-ing he admitted 'is rather risky: but I did not get ill'. Under the circumstances, such stoicism is remarkable. To climb steep mountains, day after day, subsisting on only the most basic supplies, and then having to sleep on the frozen earth with only a blanket for shelter, would have finished many a lesser individual. It was not to be much longer, however, before conditions became more comfortable. At Muli he enjoyed civilisation for the first time in weeks when he was hospitably cared for by 450 lamas in the lamasery there. It was the opportunity to take a few days well-earned rest, and take part in a lamaistic Buddhist ceremony, before continuing over the provincial border into Yunnan. At the border, the escort of Chinese soldiers that had been with him since he left Kanding returned back to their base and he was instead given twelve new soldiers to accompany him through Yunnan. The escort was four times the size of previous ones simply as a precaution against robbers.

The most challenging part of his journey was now over. He had covered a route no other Briton had, and that in itself must have been of considerable satisfaction to him. Riding mules across Yunnan, using a well-travelled trade route to the Burmese border, he 'had the luxury of inns' in which to stay. These were extremely rudimentary affairs, lacking running water, proper floors or windows, but the overnight stops he made in these remote hostelries must have indeed seemed quite luxurious after the deprivations of his march from Kanding to Muli. He finally reached Burma in mid June in a sorry state: 'I was now wearing Chinese straw sandals without socks, an old khaki suit patched … and held together with string instead of buttons, and a huge, wide-flapping straw hat.' A shopping expedition was organised with some urgency in order that he was presentable for the leisurely boat trip down the Irrawaddy to Mandalay. A month later he was residing in splendour with the Governor of Burma in his residence there. From Mandalay he travelled to Rangoon to stay with his old friend Sir Henry Blake, now Governor of Ceylon. He had not seen the Blakes since they left Hong Kong in 1903, and he had a relaxing and enjoyable holiday with them. It was there that he received the joyous news that he was to be given the permanent post of District Officer in Weihaiwei from 1 October.

His high spirits were apparent when he arrived back in Weihaiwei in October 1906, almost ten months after his departure. At Port Edward there was a joyful reunion with Stewart Lockhart, and an even warmer welcome from the Commissioner's wife, Edith, whom Reginald had not seen since her departure from Hong Kong in 1902. Edith, who was always the perfect hostess, insisted on Johnston staying with them at Government House for a few days before he set off into the countryside to establish his new life as a permanent officer in the Weihaiwei Government.

Johnston, as District Officer for the southern division, oversaw the administration of its 100,000 inhabitants. To assist him he had messengers, an interpreter (despite his protests that none was required), a clerk, eight policemen and a sergeant. He lived in the centre of the division where the Government had been given, free of charge, a group of buildings. These were the property of the Weihaiwei Gold Mining

Company, and were ideal for Reginald, being sufficiently large for him to be able to establish not only living quarters but also a court and a small police station.

Johnston was blissfully happy in his new situation, which says much for his powers of survival. His living quarters might have been stone built and extensive but, like the other buildings in the countryside, they lacked running water and plumbed sanitation. He accepted this situation without demur. Only the lack of light to read and write by, dependent as he was on supplies of candles and lamps, ever seems to have inconvenienced him. As far as he was concerned, so long as the house was clean, reasonably warm, and quiet, he had little to complain about. His books and belongings, many of them brought out of long-term storage in Hong Kong, filled his quarters. At last, he had all the contact with Chinese people that he could desire. He also had peace in the evenings to study. Writing to Loveday, he announced that he was 'very much happier and more content than I ever was or could be in Hong Kong'. But it was a lonely life. He even confided to Loveday that he had yet to fall in love, 'nor have I formed any liaison with any Oriental damsels. Many men do, of course: but I have kept away from that kind of thing without much difficulty'. With his rather monastic lifestyle he lived in as Chinese a fashion as possible, eating only Chinese food and using chopsticks, much to the alarm of European guests.

The peacefulness of his existence gave him the opportunity to pursue intellectual interests to an extent which had not been possible previously. John Murray, a publisher whose list included many of the most interesting and informative travel books on the market, agreed to publish Johnston's account of his previous year's journey. He began writing the book almost as soon as he moved to his new quarters, and also 'dabbled', as he was later to describe it, in the study of Buddhism, poetry and philosophy. The only pastime he could not indulge there was music, but even this lack was compensated by attending the odd musical evening at Government House. In his lonely, quiet little house he seems to have found a contentment which he had never felt before.

Life was abruptly disrupted in September 1907 when the Weihaiwei

Gold Mining Company went into liquidation, forcing Johnston from his cosy home. The Government had been planning to build him new quarters in due course, but these plans were barely started when the crisis came. So, until new quarters could be built or found, Johnston moved into a nearby temple. There was less space here, and his office had to double as a courtroom. This was hardly ideal, and he might have protested had he realised that this uncomfortable arrangement was to exist until 1908 when he finally moved to his permanent base in the little village of Wenchuantang.

By the spring of 1908, *From Peking To Mandalay* was ready for publication and he was actively casting round for a subject for a subsequent book. He had already decided to spend his next leave exploring central and southern China, where a number of the sacred mountains were situated, and he decided to turn this experience into a publication.

He began his next leave by visiting the mountain Wutaishan, in Shanxi Province, to the south of Beijing. In many ways this was not an exploration, as his previous journeys had been, but rather more a pilgrimage, aware as he was that he would reach some of the oldest and holiest places in China. Wutai is one of the most sacred of the Buddhist mountains. A cluster of five peaks almost 10,000 feet above sea level, it has several temples which Johnston planned to explore when he arrived there. Although there was much to see on the mountain, Johnston was later rather dismissive of the place. This may have been because the sight of Wutai was quite overtaken by his other great experience on the mountain; a private audience with the leader of Tibet's Buddhists, the Dalai Lama. He wrote about it with glee to Stewart Lockhart:

The great event so far has been my private audience with the Dalai .... The necessity of providing presents caused some embarrassment: but fortunately I had brought along a few things to give away as presents, so I did not present myself quite empty-handed. I also had to buy a ceremonial silk scarf – a Tibetan custom. The interview was thoroughly satisfactory. No one else was present except a lama who interpreted from my Chinese into the Dalai Lama's Tibetan, – and a few other lamas of high rank. He is treated here with the most unbounded reverence. I received a few presents in exchange – much more valuable than mine; including long strips of Tibetan cloth out of which winter curtains might be made, and some bundles of a peculiar kind of incense. At the end of the interview a white silk scarf was placed gracefully around my shoulders and I walked out of the room backwards with it on. Since the interview the Dalai Lama has sent every day to enquire after my health (which bears up wonderfully) and has insisted upon receiving a written epitome of my past career and my present occupation and place of abode, and also urgently demands a photograph!

Religion was to remain the predominant theme of the journey as Johnston travelled from one religious site to the next:

I have already done Hengshan in Anhui, and Songshan in Henan. In about 3 days I expect to get to Huashan: and from Hankou I shall go to Hunan and visit southern Hengshan. That, with Taishan already visited, will complete the Five Sacred Hills: and by the time I finish up I expect to have done Jiuhuashan in Anhui, Tiantai and Putuoshan, besides Wutai and Xiao Wutai.

In addition to climbing the mountains, he saw many other sights along the way. He collected rubbings from ancient monuments for himself and Stewart Lockhart whenever he could. Many of these are still in the Stewart Lockhart Collection in Edinburgh where they provide an invaluable record of numerous architectural relics which did not survive the ensuing decades of unrest in China.

Throughout this journey, and during many successive ones, Johnston stayed in temple buildings. Built in the Chinese style with simple tile roofs and their characteristic sweeping eaves, temples were usually constructed of stone. Inside, the accommodation was generally sparse. Mud or stone floors were the order of the day, and beds were more often than not a solid base set above heated pipes. Sometimes he was lucky and near the end of his journey he found particularly fine accommodation on the island of Putuo. Even today, Putuo is a favourite spot for tourists, drawing thousands of people to its shores each year. This small island, not far off the coast from Ningbo, is only about four miles long. Its hilly profile is dominated by the Buddha's Peak, which rises to 1000 feet. Part of its popularity is its dedication to the goddess of mercy, Guanyin; but another part of its enormous attraction is the sheer beauty of the place. It certainly captivated Johnston. With almost 100 monasteries and temples to explore, he knew after his first visit that a week was not long enough for Putuo and it was a place to which he was happily to return.

By the end of the year he was ready to begin writing. He found the perfect site in which to work, a monastery near Fuzhou, at Gushan, where he busily collated the mass of notes he had acquired in the previous six months. He was so immersed in this research that much of the rest of the world passed him by. It was with reluctance that he left the quiet monastery near Fuzhou. On arriving in Shanghai, Johnston received an order to go to Jinan to accompany the Commissioner on one of his favourite visits, a meeting with the Governor of the Province. A visit to Jinan with Stewart Lockhart was a rare treat, and it gave them both the opportunity to spend some time riding together and catching up with all the news they had been unable to share during his long absence from the territory. Rather as a bonus, he knew they would both be royally entertained there.

For three days, the Chinese Governor entertained Johnston and Stewart Lockhart in enormous style. The two men then set off on an extended journey through Shandong Province to Beijing. Although Stewart Lockhart cited this month-long journey as being official business, it was in fact little more than an excuse for them to have a vacation. From Jinan they rode to the Grand Canal, where boats transported them to Tianjin. There they were the guests of a former Governor of Shandong Province, Yang Shixiang, who was now Viceroy of Anhui. Nothing was too much trouble for the Viceroy who even provided the Scots with a private railway car for their journey from Tianjin to Beijing. For Johnston, accustomed to travelling on whatever rudimentary local transport was available, this was luxury indeed.

Johnston and Stewart Lockhart reached Weihaiwei at the beginning of May 1909. Johnston moved back to Wenchuantang to resume his duties as District Officer and to write his next book. However, instead of completing the sacred hills book, he began writing about quite a different subject: Weihaiwei. During his travels to the various Buddhist monasteries on the sacred hills he had acquired an enormous mass of information. Books on Buddhism, history and folklore had been purchased with tremendous enthusiasm and packed off to Weihaiwei. On his return, they quite overwhelmed him with their scale. Before too long he realised that the sacred hills would be a subject which would occupy more than a winter's work and fill more than one volume. Then Stewart Lockhart planted the suggestion of a book about Weihaiwei in his mind. As an encouragement, the Commissioner offered to provide him with a considerable amount of information about the area. Certainly, his vast knowledge of Weihaiwei, coupled with Johnston's own, meant that the book could be written relatively quickly, without much additional research. Johnston began writing in earnest in the summer of 1909, and the manuscript was completed in record time and presented to his publishers by the end of that year. John Murray published it the following year under the title *Lion and Dragon in Northern China*. It is some measure of Johnston's capacity for hard work that he wrote the 130,000-word manuscript in less than six months while doing his own time-consuming work.

Lion and Dragon in Northern China was well received by critics and the public. To this day it remains the most readable and informative book on an area which is now a forgotten part of Britain's imperial past. As with his previous book, in which he combined a travelogue with a serious academic study, the Weihaiwei book is multi-faceted. Johnston's skill lies in weaving together the various strands of Weihaiwei's character. The geography and history of the area are thoroughly discussed, and British rule explained with clarity. Johnston early discovered that the territory's charm lay in its quaint rural traditions and he makes great play of the fact that Weihaiwei had a sociological importance because of this very backwardness. Folk practices long lost in other parts of China could still be found in early twentieth century Shandong, and some lost even in rural Shandong could still be found in Weihaiwei. It is for this reason that he devoted fascinating chapters to village life and custom, the folklore of the territory, and the people of the area. Finally, he used some of the information he had gathered on the religions of China and related this to Weihaiwei.

Despite the tedium of his work, Johnston continued to find much to enjoy about Weihaiwei. Throughout 1910 he received a stream of visitors at his new base in Wenchuantang, and he and Stewart Lockhart spent many a happy hour discussing knotty sinological problems. In his spare time he continued to write like a man possessed. No sooner had the manuscript of the Weihaiwei book left his hands than he began his next book, the strangely titled *A Chinese Appeal concerning Christian Missions*. His shorthand title for this was far more suitable: *The Blast*. Written from a Chinese point of view, he used a Chinese pseudonym, Lin Shaoyang, when it was published. It denounced many missionary practices in China, reflecting views held by many educated Chinese.

It was the missionaries' belief, as he saw it, in their own cultural superiority over the Chinese which he objected to and which inspired him to write *The Blast*. The missionaries wanted to change Chinese society and this attitude infuriated Johnston. Brought up in the Anglican traditions of the Scottish Episcopal Church, Johnston loathed, as he saw it, the hypocrisy of all Christian churches. Despite the Christian creed of forgiveness, he had seen his brother lose his job in the church as a result of his father's misdemeanours. Johnston, bruised by such events, had little time for the Christian ethic. The evangelising of the missionaries and their 'meddling' – in his view – with Chinese culture were treated by him with similar disdain. *The Blast* was a devastating attack on missionary practices and was fiercely opposed by missionary groups when it was eventually published in 1911. Johnston derived no small amount of pleasure at the notoriety caused by the publication of his book. At the time there was a great deal of speculation as to exactly who was the mysterious Lin Shaoyang: the Chinese writer who could read elaborate theological tracts in both English and French. Johnston finally wrote to the *Spectator* magazine acknowledging that he was indeed British and not Chinese, although he did not reveal his true identity.

In 1911, Johnston wrote to the Colonial Office to ask for a promoted post outside the territory. He had been stuck at the same level in the service for several years and had seen contemporaries like Clementi receive advancement while he languished in Weihaiwei. In his heart of hearts, however, he knew that the response from the Colonial Office for an improved posting would be a negative one. While he waited for a reply he started to look for other posts that would take him out of Weihaiwei. Stewart Lockhart gave him every support and encouragement in these moves. Having suffered for years at the hands of the Colonial Office, the Commissioner realised that the territory was little more than a promotional graveyard for the officers serving there.

Stewart Lockhart's view was that Johnston should leave the service completely and settle for a life in academia. It was to this end that he suggested Johnston as a candidate for the post of Vice-Chancellor of the newly opened university in Hong Kong. He did so with ringing praises. 'In Mr Johnston there exists a rare combination of a man of affairs, who has proved himself an efficient and able administrator and organiser: a scholar, who is devoted to literature and philosophy and who is able to clothe his thoughts and experiences with the charm of style.' Unfortunately, the praises fell on deaf ears and it was to be years before Johnston's luck would change.

The latter part of 1911 was to end with some surprises in Weihaiwei. On 10 October, troops in Wuchang mutinied against the Emperor. Although the troops of the ruling Qing Dynasty quickly resumed control, the Wuchang uprising was sufficient to start the inexorable move towards the fall of the dynasty and the end of a monarchy in China. Within a month, Johnston was surmising that as 'Mrs W has openly declared for the Rebels ... the imperial cause is now hopeless'. Although no other historians have traced the fall of the Qing Dynasty to the fictitious Mrs Walkinshaw's affiliations, Johnston was to be all too correct in his assessment of the monarchy's demise.

If Johnston found anything to say about the revolution, it was in terms of its future potential for China. He had no great hopes of any fast solutions appearing during the first few years of the revolution and he retained this view as he watched the chaos that the overthrow of the dynasty brought in its wake. By the beginning of 1912, with Sun Yatsen declared President, it was clear that there was such a groundswell of support for the republicans that the monarchy would end, and so it was with little surprise when he heard that the boy-emperor, Puyi, had abdicated in February of that year. In the meantime, revolution arrived in Weihaiwei.

Weihai City was a peculiar anomaly within the British held territory of Weihaiwei. Under the terms of the original lease, the little walled city situated next to Port Edward remained under Chinese rule, levying Chinese taxes and under Chinese law. The only exception to this was if the security of the territory was threatened, in which case the British had the right to enter the city. In fact, Weihai and her magistrates had lived in peaceful coexistence with the British author-ities ever since civil rule had been established.

Zhao Dingyu was the Chinese magistrate in charge of Weihai City. He was a quiet, scholarly man who was well liked by Stewart Lockhart and Johnston. It was therefore with some alarm that they heard on the evening of 23 January that Zhao had been placed under close arrest by the members of the revolutionary government based in nearby Wendeng. Johnston did not hesitate to take action. Accompanied by Inspector Crudge and a small party of policemen, he entered Weihai and insisted on seeing Zhao, despite the protests of the revolutionaries. The rebels had threatened to torture Zhao unless he handed over all government monies to them, tiny though this amount was. Zhao was understandably most relieved when Johnston arrived to escort him out of the city to the safety of Port Edward. Leaving a group of armed police to guard Zhao's yamen, Johnston ordered the rebels to appear before him in court the following morning. It was an extraordinary action for a British official to take on Chinese soil.

Johnston reported all of this in a lengthy despatch to the Colonial Office. Not surprisingly, the report caused no small amount of consternation when it reached London. Officials were horrified to think that a British official had entered Chinese territory with an armed escort, and could only bless their luck that the situation had been resolved without bloodshed. Despite anxiety over Johnston's actions, he was praised for his quick response. Back in Weihaiwei, Johnston was apparently blissfully unaware that he might so easily have caused an international incident, but even if he had done it is doubtful whether this knowledge would have changed his actions.

Weihaiwei's moment of revolutionary drama was light relief compared to what was happening on the borders of the territory. From the beginning of 1912 the area was troubled by piracy. This was not the only crime Weihaiwei had to contend with, for armed robbers were also marauding along her borders. By February the situation had become so grave that Stewart Lockhart had to wire London to ask for troops to be stationed in Weihaiwei. The unsettled situation was merely a foretaste of what was to become the norm for China over the next few years.

In spite of all the unrest in China, Johnston's mood for part of 1912 was remarkably light. For the first time since he had moved to the territory he fell in love. For much of that summer, Mary, the Commissioner's daughter, had a friend – a fellow songstress – called Alice Walter staying with her. A slender, dark-haired beauty, Alice entertained the parties at Government House in the evenings with her enchanting singing voice. German Lieder were her particular forte and it was not unnatural that Johnston, who had always loved music, should be in regular attendance at these parties. Before long, he was besotted with Alice, and Mary Stewart Lockhart openly encouraged this attachment.

As was customary at this period, both girls were strictly chaperoned, but Johnston was a trusted friend of the Stewart Lockharts and there were therefore times when he did manage to see Alice on her own. The story of their romance is most tellingly revealed in Alice's diaries and by a few poems Johnston wrote to her. Although he was 17 years her senior, this difference had little effect on their relationship. The two of them exchanged letters and would sneak away together to the Chinese cemetery behind Government House to compose poetry. They both had an enormous sense of fun and their enjoyment of shared pleasures was interspersed with moments of high romance. They were realistic enough to know that their relationship had no real future and that, in Alice's own words, 'there must be a sev'rance of our ways'. She left Weihaiwei to pursue her singing career in Paris, and Johnston, who was not one to pine, must have fondly remembered their summer together for some time after.

At the end of that summer, Johnston moved back to his base in the countryside. Safely settled in Wenchuantang, he took advantage of the lack of distractions to continue to work like a man possessed on his great book on the sacred hills. The manuscript that he completed at the beginning of the following year was more than 300,000 words long: a testament to his love affair with China. This attitude, however, was being misconstrued back in Britain. His reluctance to return there was now being questioned at the Colonial Office. There, officials had already noted that he was 'a man who likes living in the wilds (He spends all his leave in the interior of China)', and concluded that Weihaiwei was therefore the perfect posting for him.

Given his apparently implacable refusal to consider a return to Britain, it is astonishing that he wrote to Stewart Lockhart in 1912 to announce that he might go to England for a few months in the autumn of 1913. He gave no explanation for this decision, although he hinted that he might see if there were any academic openings for him in Oxford. Perhaps it was the joint pressures from his old Oxford tutors and his publisher which persuaded him that to pay a visit to England would be a sensible thing to do.

Before he could take his leave, he had to finish proofing the text of *Buddhist China*, the fruits of his sacred hills research. Even for a supportive publisher like John Murray, the massive manuscript Johnston presented was too much and several chapters were cut in an effort to bring the book down to a more manageable size. Johnston was surprisingly sanguine about Murray's decision: 'My book was much longer than I thought – no wonder it took a long time to write – and if it was all printed it would cover nearly 700 pages! However, the omitted chapters will not be wasted, as they will go into a second Buddhist book.' That book was never to be written. The size of the subject was always unmanageable, and Johnston's desire to revisit all the mountains before completing it eventually halted the project in its tracks forever.

With the book out of his way, he decided to spend a few weeks in China before starting his long journey home. Until 1913 Johnston had encountered few real difficulties in travelling wherever he wanted to go, but this time the revolution thwarted his plans several times. The canal, river and railway networks were disrupted and it was only by journeying on foot and horseback that he eventually reached his destination, Putuo, in August.

Johnston completed his leave in China by staying in a temple outside Beijing that he had rented from one of the officers in the British Legation. Despite being so close to Beijing, living there was cheap and therein lay much of the attraction for Johnston: 'It is quite possible on my return from Europe next spring I may come and live in one of these temples for a year or so pending final arrangements as to where to make my home.' But before that could happen, he had to venture out of the East for the first time in 15 years.

His arrival in London in October 1913 was not auspicious: 'I find London depressing and gloomy, and I cannot say that I feel any of the pleasant emotions which I suppose one should feel on revisiting the Homeland after an absence of fifteen years. Perhaps when I get more accustomed to things I shall feel happier: but at present I feel like a fish out of water.' His demeanour was not improved by the welcome he received from his employers. Still harbouring hopes that the Colonial Office might just find him another posting, he visited the offices in Whitehall on his second day in Britain. He was alarmed, and felt rather snubbed, when he was refused even a brief meeting.

Johnston's mood was only lifted slightly when he was later sent a note asking him to attend a meeting at the Colonial Office on 9 December. He had a week before the meeting and so, in an attempt to shake off the depressive nature of London, he decided to visit his old haunts in Oxford. The visit was a revelation.

As soon as I arrived here, after fifteen years absence, I felt overwhelmed by all sorts of conflicting feelings. The climax came when I went to chapel yesterday evening. I don't want any further evidence as to the existence of ghosts – they crowded round me: – ghosts of vanished undergraduates, vanished choristers and vanished dons. The choir sang an anthem which I often heard them sing of old: it is taken from Schumann's Requiem .... I shut my eyes and the fifteen years of my life in China vanished like a dream .... Altogether, the experience was both painful and pleasurable – quite impossible to describe .... In spite of my fifteen years of prosaic life as a government official, the emotional side of my personality is by no means dead'.

After the joy of his return to Magdalen, he was rudely brought back to earth at his meeting with the Colonial Office. He met merely the Chief Clerk, who was called Harris, and 'told him that we have been badly treated at Weihai, but he seemed to regard that as a joke! .... I told him *1*. that I did not want to go back to Weihai; *2*. that I did not want to go to Hong Kong; *3*. that I did not want to leave China. He looked rather perplexed (very naturally) and appeared to regard me as a harmless lunatic'. In response, Johnston was told that he and Stewart Lockhart were 'regarded as permanent fixtures at Weihai'. More than ever, he was determined to leave the service and retire to some sleepy corner of China. Indeed, he was so disgusted with the attitude of the Colonial Office that he decided that there was no further point in remaining in London and booked a passage back to China on a ship which left in the middle of January 1914.

It was clear to him that his visit to Britain had been of little value. True, he had met several friends whom he had not seen since going to Hong Kong, including Armitage from the Magdalen 'stair'. He visited Oxford on three occasions and caught up with the academic happenings of his old college, but he had achieved little else. No attempt was made to contact his family, although he did get in touch with his lawyers, the Robertsons. One consolation was that he saw the reviews of *Buddhist China* as they appeared in the press, instead of two months later as happened when he was in China.

Reviewers were unanimous in their praise of the book, to Johnston's quiet satisfaction. However, although the book was welcomed in 1914 as a useful addition to both Chinese and religious scholarship, the estimation of its value has fared less well with the passing of time. He was dealing with a subject then known to only a few specialists, and the book, speckled with Chinese characters and obscure references, is not an easy read. His chapters on the development of Buddhism in China are rambling, to the extent at times of being uninformative, and the end result lacks the flair of his earlier books.

The sea journey back to China revived Johnston's spirits to a remarkable extent. This may have been due to the fact that he met a woman whom he mentions only as 'Dorothy' on board the ship. He fell head over heels for her, writing that 'the most beautiful name in the world is "Dorothy".' Everything seemed to be moving in the right direction for him, and he was to astound Stewart Lockhart with the news in March 1914 that relations with Dorothy had reached the stage where he was proposing marriage to her. He was quite reluctant to tell his friend any more at this stage: 'All I can say at present, for your private information, is that the girl is English, has no money, and is much too young for an elderly man like me.'

They disembarked at Hong Kong then travelled together to Beijing where life with Dorothy was a revelation for Johnston. He continued to keep her full identity his own affair, although when he met Edith Stewart Lockhart and her second daughter, Margaret, that March in Beijing he told them a little more about her. Dorothy was travelling to China to marry someone else when she met Johnston. This was probably the reason why his proposal of marriage was refused by her; a rejection which was indeed hard for him to bear. Deeply upset, he returned to Weihaiwei and closeted himself in the guest quarters of Government House. Almost ten years later her rejection still caused him pain and he wrote poignantly of how he 'was very fond of her then and still am. She married someone else: and the worst of it is she is very sorry for herself now and is very unhappy. She lives in China. I haven't told anyone else this … I should have loved to have children'.

On 4 August 1914, Britain declared war on Germany. Only four days after war was declared, Johnston was to note 'that both the German and English fleets are on the high seas – apparently looking for each other!' The interest in the area was of course concentrated on the navy as Weihaiwei was the summer base for the British China Squadron which set sail for the open seas as soon as war broke out. During those first few weeks Johnston went out every evening to search the sea for signs of action. 'I hope our ships are a match for the Germans out here,' he noted, at a time when the idea of 'trouncing the Hun' still caused huge excitement. Stewart Lockhart's son, Charles, was serving at sea and Johnston's attempt at words of comfort summed up the general mood at the beginning of the war: 'I hope he will cover himself with glory. Many doddering old animals who are now on the retired list and never saw a naval fight in their lives must envy people like Charles!' All thoughts of glory were to be shattered before too long.

Within months it was clear that the war would not be won overnight. News started to trickle into Weihaiwei, where there was an increasingly sombre mood as the enormous casualties suffered in Europe began to be known. The personal anguish of many was brought home most vividly by the letters Mary Stewart Lockhart received from her friends in London. They wrote of a whole generation of young men being killed and of their own grief as they became widows or lost their fiancées. Mary was herself affected by the war. Stuck in Weihaiwei, her plans to train in Paris were aborted. Stewart Lockhart likewise was forced to forgo the company of his wife: Edith and Margaret had reached Britain just before the outbreak of war and were forced to remain there for the duration.

In Weihaiwei, 1915 slipped seamlessly in to 1916. The war continued unabated, as did the machinations of the northern and southern factions in China, but little affected the territory or the men working there. The court work went on much as it had done for years: villagers continued to argue about land and matrimonial conflicts continued to cause trouble. Small matters like these were all Johnston and his Commissioner had to break up the monotony of life in the territory during the war. It was a strange existence. At a time when literally millions of young men were being slaughtered on the battle-fields of Europe, Weihaiwei slumbered on as though it was not a part of the rest of the world.

It was with no real sadness that Johnston heard of his mother's death in June 1916. With Noney in England, and Teddy and Reginald overseas, it was left to the family lawyer, Robertson, to make all the necessary arrangements. Reverend Black, the minister of Christ-church, took the service at which only a handful of people were in attendance. Of Isabella's children, only Noney was at the graveside. The simple ceremony could not have been in greater contrast to that held for Isabella's husband 14 years earlier. In the weeks following the funeral, Robertson settled Isabella's affairs on behalf of her family. Winding up the estate was a sad affair. All Isabella's jewellery had been pawned and her outstanding debts used almost all the money that Robertson had been holding on her behalf. Johnston covered all the additional expenses, paying for the redemption of a ring Noney expressed a desire to own. Teddy redeemed the brass carriage clock which the choir of Christchurch had given his father so many years before. Reginald wanted nothing. In his mind, a chapter had been firmly closed. Noney made one last attempt to contact him, because she 'felt sort of lonely now that Mother was away with both him and Teddy abroad'. She asked him to at least write to her. His reply was curtly similar to that given to Teddy six years earlier – 'that he didn't see the use of beginning a correspondence now that we were in Middle Age.'

The war brought many changes for Johnston and even his resolutely bachelor lifestyle at Wenchuantang was affected. People working in Hong Kong and China were now unable to get back to Britain for their leaves. Instead, they descended on Weihaiwei where they could at least enjoy the seaside. Apparently vast numbers of these visitors – in Johnston's estimation – eventually gravitated to his house, much to his chagrin. His cherished solitude was interrupted several times by guests during the summer of 1916. This not only caused him personal inconvenience; it brought huge domestic problems too. Still surviving on a basic diet of Chinese food, he did not seem to mind how he lived. While he might have been blessed with an iron constitution, he was obviously wary of subjecting any guests to the same risks as he took daily. A cart could bring him fresh supplies from Port Edward, but this journey took five hours and in the heat of summer ensured that any meat or fish was 'off' by the time it had arrived at Wenchuantang. Tinned rations were therefore what most guests were given, and any treats such as cakes they were expected to bring themselves from Port Edward. Despite this, many people were still prepared to make the journey to see him. A number did not try to make a second visit, having 'been fed on nothing but sausages and bovril'.

At the end of 1916 Johnston was forced to leave Wenchuantang and move back to Port Edward as the Consular Service could no longer spare men to help in the territory. The social situation he had endured during the previous summer was to be no better when he was based in the capital. There, even if he was not entertaining in his own residence, he had to attend Government House dinners, and these followed the formality which was expected in any British seat of government overseas. It was a particularly hot summer in 1917, and this did little to improve Johnston's temper. One evening he appeared to be particularly distracted; so much so that Stewart Lockhart enquired the next day whether he was feeling all right. Johnston's note of reply assured him that everything was fine as far as his constitution was concerned. The cause of his distraction was far more serious: 'I have come to the conclusion that what is ruining the British Empire is not the Germans but our suicidal conventions! And of those conventions our CEREMONIAL ATTIRE is one of the most calamitous!' The combination of endlessly large amounts of European food plus starched collars was becoming too much for him.

In addition to his own work, Johnston took advantage of his presence in Port Edward to try to ease some of the burdens the Commissioner bore. Stewart Lockhart was becoming increasingly prone to illness, whether it was simple colds or gout. His health became even frailer when his daughter Mary was taken to Shanghai to undergo abdominal surgery. The operation was a success, but her convalescence was protracted and Stewart Lockhart, left in Weihaiwei without his wife to help him, fretted badly. It was with some relief that he allowed Johnston to persuade him to apply for some leave in order to give Mary a holiday when she recovered.

Stewart Lockhart's absence from the territory gave Johnston his first opportunity to act as the officer in charge. He seems to have enjoyed the temporary promotion, even though it meant that he had to rise particularly early to attend to his own work before going to the Commissioner's office each afternoon to undertake duties there. In addition, he had to attend all the social functions that were normally Stewart Lockhart's task. Despite his previous grievances regarding formal dinners, Johnston now discovered that he rather enjoyed being the host: 'I gave a dinner-party to 16 people on Xmas night, and I have two other dinner-parties next week .... I am also giving a children's party on January 2nd! After that I shall have entertained the whole foreign community (including the missionaries!).' Johnston's idea to hold a party especially for the children is not surprising. He had always been very successful with them. When the Stewart Lockhart offspring were young, he had entertained them with endless stories. In Beijing, during his visits to the British Legation, he was noted for organising games of football for the children there. To their delight, he would often pretend that he was too old and unfit to last the full game.

Johnston also took the Commissioner's official paperwork in his stride, taking the opportunity of his elevated position to unleash 'a flood of information as to the general unsatisfactoriness of our administration in Weihaiwei to the Colonial Office'. Within a matter of months, Whitehall was noting 'that the real needs and circumstances of the Territory have never been properly explained, and that this is a reason why so much that ought to have been done long ago has been left undone'. Neither did Johnston temper his messages with diplomatic phrases. One official was to note, having read one of Johnston's dispatches, that 'owing to the economy of the Home Govt. administration in WHW was a disgrace to the British Empire and that the inhabitants wd. be at least as well off if they lived in China'. Given that China was by that time falling apart at the hands of various warlords, this was rather an exaggeration on Johnston's part, but his strong words at least succeeded in making the Colonial Office give some thought to the territory for the first time in years.

The first sign of a new official attitude towards Johnston was the award of a CBE in the spring of 1918. It was a lower award than that given to Clementi, but at least it was some sort of recognition for all his work and he received it with pride when it was presented to him by Stewart Lockhart who returned to Weihaiwei at the end of May 1918. Four months later, having just recovered from dysentery, Johnston took some leave, travelling to Putuo to recuperate. He moved to Shanghai in November where he heard that Germany had surrendered. He was as delighted as anyone with the allied victory. He joined in the celebrations and for several days revelled 'in the whirlpool of Shanghai society', thankful that the slaughter was finally over. Stewart Lockhart understood Johnston's euphoria, and had even greater cause to celebrate. His son, Charles, had served in the navy throughout the war and emerged unscathed, and his wife and Margaret managed to get back to Weihaiwei before the end of the year. Few British families were so fortunate, and Stewart Lockhart counted his blessings.

For British people all around the world, the ending of the war must have felt like a new beginning. For Johnston it should have given him the opportunity to decide whether or not to leave Weihaiwei once and for all. But before he had the chance to decide he was made a most tempting offer during his stay in Shanghai. The President of China had decided to appoint an English-speaking tutor for the ex-Emperor Puyi, and after some months of deliberation it was decided to offer Johnston the job. Li Jingmai, who lived in Shanghai and was a confidant of the President, was deputed to make the approach to Johnston. The offer was an enormously attractive one, the salary alone being four times as much as he received as a colonial official. For years he had been looking for a post outside Weihaiwei, and now the chance of a lifetime had been presented to him.

Johnston, however tempted, could not agree to the post immediately. As a British official, he had to insist that the offer was made through official channels and he therefore asked Li Jingmai to make the offer formally through the British Legation in Beijing. While he was waiting for that to be done, he returned to Weihaiwei. A few agonising weeks passed by as the British Minister was approached in confidence about the proposed appointment. Finally, Johnston was given the best Christmas present he could have wished for when the official offer at long last came through to Weihaiwei. The telegrams were sent. Johnston was to start life in 1919 in a post beyond his dreams: Imperial Tutor.

Chapter 3
1919-1926

JOHNSTON and Li Jingmai had known each other for several years. Li, Chinese Minister to Austria from 1904 to 1907, fled Beijing for Weihaiwei in 1911 and lived there for a few weeks as a guest of Johnston's. He later settled in Shanghai, refusing all offers of a post in the republican government, even when his pro-monarchist friend, Xu Shichang, became President. Li and President Xu hoped that China would gradually move towards becoming a constitutional monarchy and wanted a foreign tutor to educate Puyi with this goal in mind. The incentives offered were considerable in return for only an estimated two or three hours of work each day. Not only was there a good salary, but also two months annual holiday, accommodation and board. During the course of his three-year contract, Johnston would be expected 'to make recommendations on all subjects which had any direct or indirect bearing on the young emperor's intellectual and moral education, even if the acceptance ... would involve drastic changes in the customs and conventions of the Manchu Court'. This aspect alone would have made the post one which Johnston would have found very difficult to refuse.

It is telling that no one involved with the selection had been at all concerned about Johnston's ability to teach a young child. True, he had a degree in Modern History, spoke fluent Chinese, and was extremely knowledgeable about Chinese culture, religion and poetry. The training he had been given by Stewart Lockhart had given him a good grounding in the finer points of Chinese etiquette, so that he was unlikely to disgrace himself in Court. On the other hand, he had no teaching experience whatsoever, nor had he any proven experience of dealing with children. Today, such attributes would be a major factor in the selection process, but in 1918 it occurred to no one associated with the Court that a tutor should be able to demonstrate experience in these areas. This omission was symptomatic of the way Puyi was treated – not as a child, but rather as a commodity. No concern was shown for the fact that Johnston might be a disaster with children. Fortunately for the young emperor, he loved them.

His arrival in Beijing on 22 February 1919 heralded the start of his new life and the occasion underlined how quickly his position had changed. The Secretary to the Chinese President met him at the station and he was then driven to one of Beijing's grandest hotels, the Grand Hotel de Pekin. After a day of rest, Johnston was 'taken to see the President and also Prince Cai Tao, one of the Emperor's uncles. I have also to call on various Imperial Tutors, and a conservative person named Shi Xu who is Minister of the Household .... I wish all these ordeals were well over'. This round of formality did little to settle Johnston's nerves and he wrote to Weihaiwei that 'I think we may confidently anticipate that I shall get the sack within ten days'.

By mid March, Johnston was ready to move into the accommodation the palace authorities had made ready for him. Situated in an area to the north of the Forbidden City it was in the Imperial City, the part of Beijing in which most palace officials lived. Built around a series of courtyards in the Chinese style, the house was large enough to hold all his books. This was no small consideration as his library had filled 48 substantial boxes when packed for transit from Weihaiwei. The house was fitted out not only with an excess of furniture, but with the luxury of electric light and a telephone. His surroundings were of sufficient grandeur for him to entertain as his first visitor no less a person than Puyi's father, Prince Chun. Before long, Johnston was acquainted with most of the Imperial Family, and particularly enjoyed the company of Prince Cai, the first prince he had met, whom he found to be both charming and intelligent and who became a regular visitor.

Born in 1906, Puyi was only two and a half years old when he became emperor following the deaths of his great aunt, the Dowager Empress Cixi, and his uncle, the Emperor Guangxu in November

1908. His father, Prince Chun, was regent but held the post for less than 40 months before Puyi was forced to abdicate in the face of the revolution. The abdication left Puyi in a peculiar position. Under an agreement made with the fledgling Government, called the 'Articles of Favourable Treatment', he lost his power but kept his title; had the run of the huge range of palaces which were the Forbidden City, but could not leave their confines; and was guaranteed a healthy annuity of several million ounces of silver (which was never paid in full). So it was that the child was brought up as his ancestors had been. The tenth Emperor of the Qing Dynasty, he was treated by his Court as the son of heaven, even though there was now no Chinese heaven to rule over.

Johnston had his first sight of the immensity of the Forbidden City on 3 March 1919. One can only guess how he felt as he moved through the endless gates and past the many palaces making up this enormous imperial complex. The sheer size must have felt overwhelming, and he later described it as entering into another world. Its countless palaces were painted, gilded and elaborately ornamented. Everywhere he saw the colour, imperial yellow: the emperor's personal colour which was used to decorate everything from roofs to Puyi's clothes. When he eventually met Puyi that day, it was a daunting occasion of considerable formality. Johnston arrived in the early afternoon at the north gate of the Forbidden City. Sweeping yellow double roofs topped this entrance. Beneath the imposing roofline he was faced with the deep red walls of the gate which were decorated with painted and gilded carving. His carriage stopped here and Johnston transferred to a sedan chair which took him across the flagged walkway which cut through the imperial gardens in the north of the city to a second gateway. This single-storey building, also topped with yellow tiles, had three arched entrances through which Johnston walked. He turned left, walked across a small courtyard, and entered the audience chamber, the Yuqing palace. Some of the palaces in the Forbidden City are vast buildings and can hold several thousand people. The Yuqing palace, by comparison, was a relatively modest affair, comprising a waiting room, courtyard, and an audience chamber that also served as the imperial schoolroom.

The buildings within the Forbidden City, whatever their size or function, are all of a similar construction. Stone floors were softened with silk carpets. Elaborately carved screens set between columns gave each hall or palace privacy. Interiors were richly decorated with carved wooden ceilings, and door frames and wall screens were equally heavily decorated. Many of the carvings were painted or gilded, and the Emperor's symbol, the dragon, was to be found everywhere. Colourful yet gloomy, architecturally very simple but disguised with heavy ornament, the buildings were as great a paradox as the emperor's own position.

The 13 year-old Puyi arrived for the meeting with Johnston in far greater style than his new tutor; in an enormous palanquin covered in yellow silk and carried by a dozen or so bearers. Johnston was dressed in top hat and tails, while Puyi and his attendants were dressed in imperial costume. The robes looked quite sumptuous, all being deeply coloured and heavily embroidered in silks. This glorious array of costume filling the painted and gilded audience chamber presented a sight of quite extraordinary splendour. In his dark and formal European clothes, Johnston could not have been a sharper contrast to the Court. This was the moment when the strangeness of the newest courtier made a deep impression on everyone there.

Johnston reported that 'on being conducted into the audience chamber I advanced towards the emperor and bowed three times. He then descended from his seat, walked up to me and shook hands in European fashion. He remained standing during the rest of this interview and asked me a few conventional questions, mainly about my official career in China. When the interview was over I withdrew to a waiting-room and was informed that the emperor wished to begin his English lessons immediately and would receive me again in a less formal manner as soon as he had divested himself from his ceremonial garments'. Puyi later recalled the ceremony in much more personal terms in his autobiography, *From Emperor to Citizen*. Having been told some terrible tales about foreigners by the eunuchs, including the fact that they carried sticks with which to hit people, the young boy was quite relieved to discover that Johnston was human:

> *I found that Johnston was not so frightening after all. His Chinese was very fluent …. He must have been at least forty at the time and was clearly older than my father, but his movements were still deft and skilful. His back was so straight that I wondered whether he wore an iron frame under his clothes …. It was his blue eyes and greying fair hair in particular that made me feel uneasy.*

There were to be other surprises when they met. Johnston was delighted to discover that Puyi was allowed to read Chinese newspapers, and had a good general knowledge of the world outside. Johnston's high standards made an impression on Puyi. The emperor soon understood that Johnston was not a man to be crossed:

> *He had only to go red in the face for my father and the high officials to give way …. I found him very intimidating and studied English with him like a good boy, not daring to talk about other things when I got bored or ordering a holiday as I did with my Chinese tutors.*

Very quickly, the Court and his fellow tutors recognised that Johnston was able to exact a far stricter discipline on the boy than anyone else could. Puyi would listen to him and later admitted that he thought 'everything about Johnston was first-rate'. Part of this attraction may well have been the fact that Johnston was probably the only person who had ever treated Puyi as a child. He could relate to Puyi's age without any trouble, writing with fondness about his 'small pupil, who shows far greater keenness about his studies than I did at his age'. The influence the Scottish tutor could bring to bear was to be used by many people in the inner circle of Court, and before long Johnston was playing the part of an imperial intermediary.

His time with Puyi was not confined, even in the first few weeks, solely to the daily lesson. One day the emperor took him to see the imperial garden, and Johnston was allowed to photograph the grounds. On other occasions Puyi would take him round the palace and show his teacher some of the thousands of works of art that adorned the rooms. The middle-aged Scottish tutor and the young Chinese boy shared something else in common which was to strengthen Johnston's position in the classroom: a sense of humour. It is not known whether or not Johnston shared his stories about The Quork and the rest with Puyi, though it is unlikely that he could have resisted the temptation to do so for long. Certainly, Puyi could display an impish talent at times and they had fun drawing caricatures together to break up the hard work of lessons.

Johnston knew how to capture a child's imagination and before too long seems to have assumed the mantle of a benevolent uncle rather than a tutor. As the boy became more and more interested in western life he even asked Johnston to give him an English name to use on non-Chinese documents. Johnston had the idea of offering him one from a list of the names used by the British royal family, and Puyi chose the name Henry which he was to use for many years after. Although the lessons quickly became wide-ranging discussions, there was one thing Johnston refused to teach Puyi: the Christian religion. When a Seventh Day Adventist called on Johnston, 'bringing with him a bag containing a number of Christian books and tracts which he wished me to bring to the notice of His Majesty', he was given short shrift.

Of course, he was not the only person to be tutor to Puyi. The emperor also had Chinese tutors and Johnston got to know these men well. There were four men in this erudite group and they held an extraordinary position of status within the Court. Traditionally, an Imperial Tutor – and this was to include Johnston even though he was a foreigner – took precedence over everyone else apart from some of the Imperial Princes. Chinese tutors therefore came from the cream of scholarly and administrative society. They were learned men of high standing and, in sharp contrast to Johnston, were all extremely elderly. All the tutors were treated equally and with lavish kindness. On their birthdays, they would receive presents from the emperor and his family and quarterly bonuses were the norm. In Johnston's case these emoluments alone were more than his annual salary as a District

Officer, bringing his income to far more than Stewart Lockhart's salary as Commissioner.

Johnston wasted no time before trying to change the environment around Puyi. He had only been in the Forbidden City for a few days when he first crossed swords with the thousands of eunuchs there. He had suspected before he even arrived in Beijing that he would have trouble with them, but even he was surprised at the speed with which this had happened. He never gave an indication as to what started his battle, but Edward Behr, in his biography of Puyi, recorded that the day Johnston met Puyi 'the court eunuchs crowded round him, congratulating him on his new appointment and demanding money on this auspicious occasion'. Johnston horrified them by reputedly asking for a receipt for anything that he gave them.

His initial concern about this formidable imperial force was the influence they had on Puyi. Johnston found the eunuchs to be shallow, obsequious and avaricious and believed that such people should not be the emperor's primary companions. It was an unhealthy situation in which to place any impressionable adolescent and Johnston was horrified with what he discovered about palace life. However, what disgusted him just as much as the eunuchs were the antics of some members of the Imperial Household Department.

Johnston quickly realised that an enormous amount of power within the Forbidden City rested in the hands of the Imperial Household Department which controlled every aspect of life there. He began to hate the department with a real passion once he understood that the eunuchs, who were part of it, were only a symptom of a far larger problem caused by the very existence of the department itself, which he likened, in *Twilight in the Forbidden City*, to 'a vampire draining the life-blood of the dynasty'. Almost a thousand officials were members of it, and he could find little good in any of them. What underpinned the corruption of the department was the system of bribes and diversion of money at every level within it. This made senior posts some of the most desirable in the country and Johnston reckoned that some officials collected more than £200,000 a year this way: a vast sum in

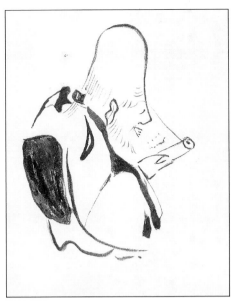

The Earl of Dumbarton reading a letter from the Quork.

Left: 'The Earl of Dumbarton reading a letter from the Quork.' A brush and ink drawing by Reginald Johnston.

Below: The Magdalen 'Stair' in 1897.

no. B. New Buildings
Magd. Coll. Oxon. c. 1897

J. P. Armitage   R. F. Johnston   T. Loveday   P. J. Dale   J. H. Wood   C. Clementi.
J. B. Lambert

Left: Johnston (on the left), Stewart Lockhart and Clementi at Government House, Weihaiwei, in 1905.

Below: Johnston and his bearers at an inn en route to Qufu with the portrait of Edward VII in 1904.

"The District Officer" Beikou Xmas 1906

Above: Johnston's quarters at Wenchuantang in 1908.

Left: A page from one of Stewart Lockhart's scrapbooks showing Johnston outside a temple at Beikou in Shandong Province, Christmas 1906.

Above: The island of Putuo, photographed by Johnston in 1908.

Below: Johnston on circuit as District Magistrate in Weihaiwei, *circa* 1906.

To Sir J.H. Stewart Lockhart
from
R.F. Johnston.

Peking:
September 1922.

Left: Johnston in his sable coat and mandarin hat, September 1922.

Below: Cherry Glen in 1921. The three figures in the doorway are (from left to right) Mr Liu, a friend of the Manchu court, and imperial tutors Chen Baoshen and Ju Yifan.

Above and left: The main building at the Summer Palace.

Below: An aerial view of Weihaiwei in 1929.

實根培埈

Above: Johnston in 1927 with his Senior District Officer and staff of the Government School in Weihaiwei, holding the scroll written by Emperor Puyi.

Below: Johnston leaving Weihaiwei for the last time in October 1930. He is holding the silver cup presented to him by the Chinese. Commander Xu is on the far right.

Left: Reginald Johnston in 1934.
The photograph was taken by
Sarah Markham, Dr Thomas
Loveday's daughter.

Below: Eilean Righ in 1934.

the early 1920s. Excess was rife. In the imperial kitchens, for example, accounts showed that, aged four, Puyi apparently consumed 240 chickens and ducks each month!

By the summer of 1919 Johnston felt he knew enough of palace life to write a letter of warning to Li Jingmai. In the strongest terms he warned 'that in my opinion the highly artificial life that the emperor leads must be detrimental to his health, physical, intellectual and moral; and I sincerely hope for his sake that some means will be devised whereby he may be enabled to live more naturally and rationally. Although he is an emperor (a titular one) he is also a boy, and if this fact is ignored, especially during the next three or four years, the results may be very serious for him'. Johnston's eloquence was to be disregarded, despite his prescient warning that Puyi was in danger of becoming a failure as a person unless the artificiality of his life was radically changed. He would hardly have been placated to learn how accurate his assessment of Puyi was to become.

Johnston was becoming incredibly fond of Puyi. He cared deeply for the child, and was justified in feeling dismayed by the activities of the eunuchs and palace officials. He was aware that few people really loved the young emperor and that the self-serving mentality which pervaded the palace could only do him harm. He despaired of Puyi's father, Prince Chun, who he felt played too small a role in his son's upbringing. He described Chun as lacking in strength of character and being terribly weak. One incident illustrates just how isolated and abandoned Puyi was. It took Johnston but a matter of weeks to ascertain that Puyi was shortsighted and needed glasses; and this in an environment where the child's every moment was apparently under scrutiny. Yet no one else, not his tutors, servants or family, had been aware of this problem because no one looked after him in any parental capacity. Johnston recommended that he saw an optician immediately, but nothing was done. As the child's sight worsened he began to suffer badly from headaches and Johnston was driven to despair. It was two years before Johnston, only by threatening to resign, finally managed to bring an ophthalmologist into the palace to examine the emperor and prescribe glasses for him. There was, of course, the predictable uproar when he brought in a westerner to rectify the problem, but by then he was well past caring what the Court thought of him.

As the weeks went by and Johnston gradually became accustomed to his new station in life, his lifestyle started to change as well. Once a frugal District Officer who was content to ride on mules if need be, he now decided that he would acquire a car of his own and before the end of 1919 was the proud owner of a five-seater Ford motor car. He took to driving across Beijing in his luxurious new vehicle, boasting that the car cut his journey time to the palace by two-thirds; quite an achievement in a crowded city not designed for motorised transport. An even bigger achievement was that he did not injure man or beast in making the journey each day.

Johnston's duties in Beijing were such that he still found time to write. Major books were not possible, due to a combination of his official duties, his plans for the emperor, and the considerable amount of socialising he was now expected to do. However, he wrote one short book and several magazine articles. His book, on Chinese drama, was little more than a sketch, partly due to time constraints and partly because he was 'not really greatly interested in the Chinese theatre'. Despite this extraordinary confession, the publishers pressed him to write it, but it was no surprise that sales were unimpressive. Most of the articles he wrote between 1919 and 1921 were for the *New China Review* under the pseudonym Christopher Irving. He wisely avoided political subjects, even under a pseudonym. Instead, he covered a mixed bag of topics, from articles on Buddhist art and on Chinese society and customs to the inevitable one or two designed specifically to annoy his old enemies, the missionaries.

As the first year of his appointment slipped by, President Xu, keen to lavish attention on the tutor, offered to purchase a property in the Western Hills for Johnston. Overwhelmed by this offer, which he knew would cost Xu thousands of dollars, Johnston eventually agreed to it on the condition that he would hold it only for as long as he lived in China. That resolved, he quickly settled on the place he wanted.

Thereafter, Cherry Glen was to be one of his most prized possessions – a place where his long-held dream of a Chinese retreat was to be realised.

When Johnston found his little haven in the Western Hills in 1920, it was only a plot of land. 'It contains a number of fruit trees, including walnut trees; and also other trees such as poplars. The scenery is beautiful. It is right in the heart of the mountains, but can be reached in five hours from Beijing. One of its greatest attractions is a mountain-stream which never runs dry and runs through the middle of the property.' Johnston loved the place from the first moment he saw it. Immediately, he arranged for a house to be built there and spent the summer of 1920 living in a tent while construction started. Cherry Glen was a substantial property covering several acres. Over the years, he turned this into his own paradise. Shrines to unknown gods and his favourite poets were erected. The Chinese temple he designed was a particularly prized spot for him.

He even installed a statue of Buddha there, which he borrowed from one of the local villages. On warm summer evenings when he was alone at Cherry Glen, he would sleep in the temple in contented solitude, wakening the next day to the chorus of songbirds that populated the grounds. After so many years of dreaming and hoping for his place in the hills, he found perfection here. He lavished money on the property, planting trees and a profusion of flowers and laying out walks and rocky viewpoints. Eventually, the grounds alone were sufficiently elaborate to require the services of four gardeners.

As the buildings and grounds developed, Johnston invited increasing numbers of guests to Cherry Glen. Some were friends from the Legation Quarter, but many others were courtiers. His fellow tutor, Chen Baoshen, was an early visitor, and in his second summer there Prince Cai and his son Pujia came and spent a few nights with him. Johnston was blissfully happy with his lot and made up his mind that when he retired he would settle in Cherry Glen. Whenever he could he would visit it, entertaining a wide variety of guests. In June 1921, a party of British people took a walking tour in the hills. Among the group was Eileen Power, an historian making her first visit to the country. Johnston was always keen to meet new and interesting characters, and so it is not surprising that Miss Power and her party were invited to spend a weekend with him in Cherry Glen. It seems to have been an immediate meeting of minds. Eileen Power certainly enjoyed her time at Cherry Glen, and several years later she and Johnston were to form a very close relationship.

Johnston was convinced that the best thing for Puyi was to get him away from the Forbidden City, and he saw a visit to Europe as an extension to the imperial education. He and Puyi spent many a happy hour planning the itinerary. However, Johnston was playing a dangerous game, and one which was finally to have catastrophic consequences for Puyi. In attempting to break the mould of the rituals of courtly life he was giving Puyi false hopes. Johnston seemed to be genuinely unaware of what he was doing. For example, he introduced the idea of a telephone to Puyi in an attempt to give him some contact with the outside world. Puyi relates in his autobiography how his request for a telephone met with a fairly predictable response from the palace: 'There is no precedent for such as thing in the ancestral code. If a telephone is installed anyone might talk to Your Majesty, a thing that has never happened in the times of your ancestors.' Puyi, with Johnston's support, was to get his phone and eventually tried to use it to make his escape from the palace.

Puyi's desire to escape from the Forbidden City was not unnatural. He had spent most of his life there and as he grew older he yearned to see the world Johnston had told him so much about. In September 1921 Johnston had to watch Puyi suffer as his mother committed suicide. They had not been close and he had been deprived of her company for most of his youth, but Puyi was allowed to make a final visit to her. This was the first time he had left the Forbidden City since becoming emperor. He travelled through streets lined with soldiers in a retinue of cars to the Northern Mansion in the city to spend half a day with his mother. It must have been a traumatic experience, for the Princess had taken an overdose of raw opium to end her life. Johnston was proud of the way Puyi conducted himself, behaving 'splendidly throughout' despite being 'very much distressed'. Johnston did his best to console him, but unfortunately did so by continuing to make much of the plans for their trip to Europe. Puyi was as eager as Johnston to leave Beijing, and his sad visit to the Northern Mansion increased his desire to travel further afield.

At the beginning of 1922 the Emperor gave Johnston a special gift which illustrated his high regard for the tutor; he appointed him Mandarin of the Second Rank with a Coral Button. The honour came complete with a sable robe, which Johnston took great delight in wearing. 'The Sable Robe is a most magnificent garment – and as large as a loose overcoat, made entirely of sable. I am told it is worth at present prices over $4000'; the equivalent of a whole year's salary for a District Officer. His mandarin's sable hat, topped with a button made from coral, was equally prized. While the Court gave one the robe, the usual practice was to purchase the button oneself. In Johnston's case, even this was given to him, by the head of the Imperial Household. It was a great honour. 'I believe high mandarin rank has been conferred on other Europeans before – Sir Robert Hart for instance – but I am told by the palace folk that the honour of being entitled to wear the sable cloak – not to mention the cloak itself – has never before been granted to a foreigner, and to very few Chinese or non imperial Manchus.' Essentially, it was an honour conferred on princes of the royal house but given to few others, and so spoke eloquently of the regard in which Johnston was held not only by Puyi but also by the Imperial Family.

Johnston took his glorious new robes off to Cherry Glen where he posed for photographs in his new guise as Mandarin. It was a proud moment, but one which marked the end of Johnston's career as Imperial Tutor. It was 18 years since he had posed so regally for the camera; the previous occasion being when he set off for Qufu with the King's portrait for Duke Kong. Then, he had been a slim, good-looking man of 29, who was as fit as a fiddle. Now he presented a very different picture. Aged 47, the years in the East had taken their toll. Although he had been blessed with remarkably robust health, his life in the Weihaiwei countryside had not been one of luxury. Johnston looked old and careworn, and could easily have been mistaken for a man in his fifties. It was several years since he had made any really taxing journeys across China, and his soft life in Beijing had turned the slim athlete into a rather stocky old man. Only the sparkling blue eyes remained the same.

The degree to which aspects of Puyi's life were predetermined for him is clearly illustrated by the decision to have him marry when he was only 16. In getting married, Puyi, who was still a child in many ways, officially became a man. Men do not need teachers or classrooms, and for many weeks following Puyi's betrothal in March 1922, Johnston prepared for an end to his imperial employment. His three years' contract as Imperial Tutor was completed and he expected to be able to start a completely new life in Cherry Glen before too long. But even with Cherry Glen to retire to, leaving the Court and his beloved Puyi would have been a wrench, and so it was to his immense satisfaction that he was informed that 'the imperial family won't hear of my resigning' and that Puyi had therefore asked him to remain on his staff.

The young woman selected to be Puyi's first wife and empress was, predictably, a member of the Imperial Family. The future Empress Wan Rong, who was the same age as Puyi, had been brought up in Tianjin with her family following the abdication, and came from a long line of Manchu aristocracy. Simultaneously, Puyi was given a secondary consort, as was the tradition. Like Wan Rong, she was a Manchu, but of far lower rank and only 14 at the time of her marriage. The customs surrounding the choice of wife and consort for Puyi were centuries old. He had little or no say in the matter himself, and was not even permitted to see his intended bride before the wedding.

Johnston must have been aware as he watched the wedding on the first day of December 1922 that he was seeing one of the great events of state. He certainly suspected – correctly as it transpired – that the sights before him would never again be seen in China. The wedding itself was a protracted affair, which began with the Empress leaving her house at three in the morning to process to the Forbidden City to be married. With an escort of soldiers, cavalry, infantry and bands, Wan Rong was also accompanied by 60 lantern bearers, 70 flag bearers, 22 chair bearers, servants, eunuchs, and officers of the household. This rich and awesome sight was followed an hour later with a smaller procession taking the consort, Wen Xiu, to the Forbidden City. There, the protracted wedding ceremony was the start of five days of festivities. It was hours before all the music, chanting and ritual of the wedding itself were over. The thousands of courtiers and officials in their gorgeous robes processing across the city, the gifts and the feasting, were all part of an elaborate performance, an arcane and archaic ritual which marked a coming of age for Puyi. It was also to be the final burst of imperial colour for Beijing.

Puyi did not forget his tutor among all the wedding festivities. As a wedding honour, Johnston was awarded a mandarin button of the highest rank, a rare honour for a courtier. He was as delighted with this as he had been with his sable cloak, but could not help noting that despite being unable to 'get anything more henceforth in the shape of buttons … the Manchus are treating me better in the way of honours than the Colonial Office!' He also treasured until his death the silver goblet Puyi gave him that day.

As Puyi moved towards marriage, his discontent with his situation grew steadily worse. There were times when the sheer pointlessness of his situation depressed him, and his inability to leave the Forbidden City added to his frustration. Johnston did his best, encouraging him to talk about the trip to Europe, and tried to get him to do something about the waste and corruption that was the hallmark of the imperial complex. It was to little avail and in the summer of 1922, only three months after his engagement, Puyi begged Johnston to take him to Europe. Johnston refused, although he yearned to free Puyi from the Forbidden City. Johnston always believed firmly in the constitutional way and could not countenance helping Puyi to flee Beijing. Perhaps most alarmingly, Puyi's plans did not include his bride-to-be. Johnston explained the matter in *Twilight in the Forbidden City* by saying that this was 'perhaps not altogether surprising ... inasmuch as Chinese and Manchu custom, not to say court etiquette, made it impossible for him to meet the empress-elect before the wedding'. It was hardly an auspicious beginning to a courtship.

Johnston may have been content with his lot, but Puyi remained as unhappy as ever. His marriage did little to pacify him and he continued to fret and to plot to leave the Forbidden City. From the outset his marriage was a strange one. He abandoned his wife on their wedding night and may never have consummated their union. Neither his wife nor consort seemed to play a significant part in his life. Indeed, in Puyi's autobiography, Johnston is mentioned more frequently than Wan Rong. Johnston tried to encourage Wan Rong, to whom Puyi had given the English name Elizabeth, to become part of the close partnership he had with the emperor. For a time in Beijing this worked. The imperial couple, with Johnston's encouragement, found time for some fun together. But despite Johnston's best attempts at improving Puyi's relationship with Wan Rong, he did not get very far. With only two serious romances in his own life, the middle-aged bachelor was hardly in a position, even if etiquette had permitted, to advise Puyi on marital matters. It did not help that Johnston had been unhappy when Puyi was married in 1922, noting that 'it is a pity they married him so young'.

After his abortive attempt to leave the imperial confines in the summer of 1922, Puyi set about planning an alternative means of escape. He had a brother, Pujie, who was slightly younger than he was. Pujie lived in his parents' house, the Northern Mansion, and therefore had more freedom of movement than his brother the emperor. The Northern Mansion had its own telephone, giving the brothers the opportunity to talk when Pujie could not visit the palace, and therefore allowing them the chance to plot an escape. For some time Prince Cai had made a house ready for Puyi in the English concession in Tianjin. Johnston knew about the house, but always hoped it would only be used when the time came for Puyi to leave Beijing legitimately. Puyi had other ideas and helped by Pujie began to move paintings, calligraphy and antiques from the imperial collections to the house in Tianjin. Having created a cache of valuables, he then planned a secret flight from the Forbidden City. Unfortunately, Pujie's trips out of the Forbidden City carrying heavily laden suitcases aroused suspicion and his own servants told his secret to Prince Chun. He had the exits from the city sealed and Puyi remained in his yellow prison.

Johnston continued to try to push Puyi towards other activities to keep him occupied and to stop him thinking of further escape attempts. Johnston had suggested to Puyi in 1922 that he reorganised the palace systems, but events such as the imperial wedding had pushed the matter into the background. Now he encouraged Puyi to look into the excesses of the Imperial Household Department, and to tackle the problem of the eunuchs.

Literally thousands of treasures were stored in rooms around the Forbidden City. Some had been hidden from sight for centuries. Others had been sold off to pay for imperial debts, but exactly what had gone was not known. The first thing to do, therefore, was to try and ascertain what still remained and where. Puyi decided to instigate an inventory of palace treasures and announced that he would begin by inspecting the Palace of Established Happiness, one of the most important treasuries in the complex. But before he had the opportunity to see what treasures were still there, the building was burnt down on the evening of 27 June 1923. Started almost certainly by disgruntled eunuchs, the great fire caused enormous damage. Johnston described the fire as 'disastrous'. He could only rue the passing of beautiful objects and valuable historical texts dating from the medieval period, far less the damage to the buildings. Literally thousands of objects were incinerated that night, and Johnston's own list details the loss of almost 3000 buddhas, over 1000 paintings, almost 2000 gold altar ornaments, porcelain, jades and bronzes as well as books and imperial robes.

Johnston was greatly saddened by the fire, but he displayed nothing but joy at its final effects: the abolition of the eunuch system. The fire gave Puyi his chance to make a move on the eunuchs, for he was furious at their treachery. On 15 July he issued an edict expelling his staff of eunuchs. He gave them but an hour's notice of his decision in order to minimise the chances of them doing any further damage in the palaces. Only the 50 eunuchs serving the three surviving dowager empresses were allowed to remain. This was a significant moment for the deposed monarch, for the expulsion of the eunuchs did more than anything else had done to signal that the Court was moving irrevocably into the twentieth century. Johnston was later to recall, with a certain amount of glee in *Twilight in the Forbidden City*, 'the unwonted spectacle of palace-eunuchs sitting in disconsolate groups on the parade-ground between the northern wall of the Forbidden City and Prospect Hill, awaiting their turn to return to the palace in twos and threes to collect their personal property'.

In his own small way, Johnston created his own memorial to the expulsion, and at the same time gave Puyi something to take his mind away from his hopeless position. It was with delight that Johnston arranged to have a recreation area built on the site of the Palace of Established Happiness, which had been demolished in the great fire. There he taught Puyi to play tennis and, in an effort to encourage Wan Rong and Puyi to spend more time together, arranged for the purchase of bicycles for both of them. Given that only a few years earlier Puyi had been carried everywhere in procession, the freedom to be able to whiz around the palaces on a bicycle must have been an enormously refreshing experience for him. He even had the steps around doorways removed so that he and Wan Rong could speed through the buildings without obstruction.

With no eunuchs to fight, Puyi began to turn his attention to a reform of the Imperial Household Department. He and Johnston decided to put a man in charge of the operation whom they could both trust; a career official, Zheng Xiaoxu. The appointment itself was a radical departure from imperial custom. Such important (and lucrative) posts were traditionally held by Manchus, but Zheng was Chinese. With no clan or family ties to hinder him, he immediately set about restructuring the department and sacking its most corrupt members. Johnston held Zheng, an old-fashioned scholar of the Confucian school, in high esteem and within three months Zheng reduced palace expenditure by thousands of dollars. These savings were not exacted, of course, without enormous opposition from the Imperial Household Department.

An obvious way to cut court expenditure further was to move Puyi to the Summer Palace. Johnston had been trying to achieve this for years, but the major obstacle to doing so had always been the Imperial Household Department. They had argued consistently that if Puyi left the Forbidden City then he would lose his imperial treasures for ever, for the Summer Palace was too small to contain all of them. Johnston did not think that that was a difficulty, and argued that if an agreement could be reached with the Government as to what were national treasures, then Puyi and his family might be left with all that remained, and that these things could go to the Summer Palace. The department then maintained that the Summer Palace was in too poor a state of repair to accommodate the emperor. Johnston shrugged this off too, by offering to have the palace redecorated. Their main objection was the one the department dared not utter, however; namely that the Summer Palace could never accommodate all the staff employed within the Forbidden City at that time. Jobs would be lost, and with them all the other perquisites the staff had enjoyed for so long. Zheng and Johnston both agreed that the only way to achieve a move to the Summer Palace was to take control of the complex away from the Imperial Household Department. Zheng therefore recommended to Puyi that Johnston be appointed Imperial Commissioner for the Summer Palace. Johnston's glee was undisguised. He positively revelled in the shock inflicted on the department by the knowledge 'that a considerable portion of the imperial domain should be wholly withdrawn from their control and placed under that of a Western barbarian'.

Some seven miles from the Forbidden City, the Summer Palace was the country retreat for the emperor. There had been a palace of some sort on the site since the twelfth century, but most of the buildings were relatively modern in date, though built in the traditional Chinese style.

Unlike the Forbidden City, which had been designed to be a giant imperial office, with each building having a specific imperial function, the Summer Palace was a pleasure ground. Almost completely surrounded by water, it was formed from a series of gardens and pavilions connected by pathways. It was designed for relaxation and, for example, boasted the largest theatre in China. The theatre typified the fantastical atmosphere of the place. Three storeys high, it was fitted with trapdoors in its ceiling and floors so that elaborate performances could take place in which supernatural creatures appeared and disappeared on the stage as if by magic. Pretty pavilions, made from carved and painted wood, offered stunning views through their fretwork of the Kunming Lake, one of the most beautiful in China. It even had the ultimate folly in its grounds; a huge marble boat sitting on the lake. The boat was a folly in more than one sense, for it is the supreme irony that funds which should have been used to improve the Chinese navy were instead diverted to build this useless extravagance. Whereas the Forbidden City was heavily ornamented and filled with buildings, the Summer Palace was a mixture of intimate buildings, gardens and rolling parkland. No wonder Johnston was so keen to move there.

If the shock of seeing the Summer Palace taken out of their control and handed over to Johnston for safe-keeping were not enough, the Imperial Household Department was soon to receive an even bigger shock. Having appointed Johnston Imperial Commissioner, Puyi then announced he wished to make a visit to the palace. There was the predictable opposition to this, but Puyi – and Johnston – stood firm, and in the spring of 1924 the emperor made his first visit outside Beijing. Puyi and Johnston headed the entourage as it made its way out of the city. Wan Rong followed in a second car. Following her was an escort of six cars filled with republican guards; and following them were another six cars, filled with officials from the Imperial Household Department. To pass through the walls of Beijing and out into the countryside was a revelation to Puyi – he discovered the joy of freedom for the first time. The day was an enormous success for everyone except the Imperial Household Department, and Puyi quelled the

Government's fears by not making an attempt to rush off to the Legation Quarter for sanctuary.

Johnston began to spend more and more time at the Summer Palace, and finally moved there for a month in August 1924. Despite his delightful surroundings, his task was not an easy one. 'It isn't all plain-sailing or holiday-making by any means. I have to contend with a great deal of unpleasant opposition, and have already been threatened (in anonymous letters) with assassination!' Undeterred, Johnston introduced outrageous practices, such as awarding contracts for building to the lowest tender – a concept quite alien to the Imperial Household Department. Buildings were repaired, rents from the adjoining farmland reviewed, fish from the palace lake sold to fish-mongers, hunting rented out and also visitors' days introduced to produce a revenue from entrance tickets. Johnston even arranged for the estate to share in the profits of some local enterprises such as an hotel, tea-houses and a photography shop. Within three months he had 'practically succeeded in wiping out the annual deficit and thereby relieving the Imperial Household of heavy expenses for maintenance'.

Having Johnston living at the Summer Palace gave Puyi the excuse he needed to leave the Forbidden City regularly. Johnston had hoped that Puyi, having proved to be reliable, might be permitted to visit the palace without an armed escort. However the government authorities insisted on keeping a close eye on him, and so each visit was made with an escort of six cars of soldiers. Twice in the summer of 1924 Puyi and Wan Rong made the trip to see Johnston, who organised lavish luncheon parties for the royal couple and had three rowing boats built especially for them. In *Twilight in the Forbidden City* he recounts how even an activity as innocent as rowing was greeted by palace officials 'with horror when they observed the Son of Heaven toiling at an oar when he might very well have left that arduous and menial occupation to his bargemen'. Breaking centuries of imperial custom was never going to be easy, but Johnston retained a dogged determination to try. Puyi proved he could leave his little yellow-coloured kingdom without causing rebellion or bloodshed and gradually the reins which had held him for so long began to be loosened slightly. Emboldened by this new freedom, he even managed a brief mountain ramble to the Western Hills with Johnston that August.

When the warlord Feng Yuxiang marched on Beijing on 22 October 1924, the Foreign Legations were thrown into a state of panic and the Legation Quarter was packed to its limit with refugees. At the same time the Forbidden City was dealing with its own small crises. A dowager empress, Duan Kang, had died at the end of October and the Court was in official mourning in preparation for her funeral. Despite this, troops surrounded the imperial compound and phone lines were cut. Johnston went to see Puyi there on 2 November and decided that somehow he had to get the emperor out of Beijing. Puyi gave him some important documents and several precious belongings which Johnston later deposited in a bank for safe-keeping. Puyi also gave him one final memento from the imperial collections, one of Duan Kang's jade rings which Johnston treasured for the rest of his life.

Johnston returned to the palace the next day, and the one after that. He found the Forbidden City to be forlorn and deserted. Once more he discussed with Puyi plans for escape. They were both unsure as to how this would be achieved as all the gates were guarded, but they continued to hope for some chink of light. That opening was never to appear. On 5 November, troops entered the Forbidden City and imprisoned Puyi. They brought with them a document for Puyi to sign, revising the original abdication agreement and giving him three hours to leave his palace. With no operational telephone he could not reach Johnston, and to make matters worse the troops would only permit Puyi's two remaining Chinese tutors and his father, Prince Chun, to see him.

Prince Chun was the last person one would have wanted in a crisis. Blubbering and senseless, he was useless to Puyi. With armed guards threatening the Court, the emperor had no options available to him. There was nothing left for it but to sign the revised articles and leave the Forbidden City for his father's house, the Northern Mansion. Escorted to the gates by armed guards, Puyi found five cars waiting to take him and his family from the palace. For the first time in almost three hundred years the Forbidden City was without a Qing Emperor.

Johnston waited until nightfall before going to the Northern Mansion. There he found Puyi to be remarkably calm, but Prince Chun was in his characteristic state of panic. Although he did his best to raise the spirits of the Imperial Family, and especially those of Puyi, Johnston admitted that by the end of that day on 5 November he was 'anxious and despondent'. He did not see Puyi for another three weeks.

Feng Yuxiang's triumph was short lived and he was overthrown by a rival warlord within the month. The new Government immediately removed all restrictions on Puyi's movements, giving Johnston the chance to visit him. Johnston decided to act swiftly to free Puyi, although he had no authority or any real support for any action within the British Legation. Nevertheless he arranged to get Puyi out of the Northern Mansion and into the German Hospital in the Legation Quarter, where Puyi could stay until a Legation was found which would harbour him.

They made their move on 29 November. Johnston arranged to have Puyi's car ready at the gates of the Northern Mansion on the unlikely pretext of going for a short drive with him. In order to allay any fears of an escape, Wan Rong was left behind, with Johnston promising to get her to the Legations later. All seemed to be going well until two armed guards jumped onto the car's running boards as it left the mansion. Stuck with these unwelcome companions, Johnston instructed the chauffeur to drive to a photography shop which was in the Legation Quarter on the pretext that he and Puyi wanted to buy some supplies. When they reached the shop the guards remained with the car, making no comment about the shopping expedition. Johnston and Puyi made some purchases and when they left the shop Johnston suggested that they should visit an old friend, Dr Dipper, as they were in the vicinity of the German Hospital. Unbelievably, the guards did not follow them on the short walk. Safely inside the hospital, Puyi was ushered into an empty ward where Johnston left him in the care of a German doctor while he went to seek help from the Legations.

Johnston's actions caught the diplomats in the Legations completely by surprise. Three weeks had passed since Puyi's expulsion from the Forbidden City. During that time, Johnston had visited the Legation Quarter daily, and he must have known that he had absolutely no guarantee that any Legation would offer Puyi sanctuary. Presumably he believed that, with Puyi in the Quarter, someone in the diplomatic corps would be compelled to offer him a safe haven. The fates did not seem to be smiling on his venture. He went to the Dutch and Japanese Legations, but the Ministers were out. He then turned to the British Legation where Macleay, the British Minister, told him what he feared to hear: 'It has never been the practice of this Legation to receive political refugees.' Johnston was becoming desperate. He finally judged that he should return to the Japanese Legation, because he knew they had a history of admitting political refugees.

While Johnston was frantically visiting the Legations, Puyi was becoming increasingly anxious. Finally, his old Chinese tutor, Chen Baoshen arrived at the German Hospital with Zheng Xiaoxu, the man Puyi had put in charge of the Imperial Household Department. They recommended, possibly for the same reasons that Johnston favoured the Japanese Legation, that Puyi should go there. Worried about the time Johnston was taking to return with news, and terrified that at any minute his father would turn up and halt his plans to escape, Puyi took their advice. As Puyi was making his way to the Japanese Legation, Johnston was meeting the Minister there and asking for sanctuary for him. After some thought the Minister gave his consent, and Johnston rushed back to the German Hospital, only to discover that Puyi had already left to go to the Japanese Legation. It was an afternoon in the traditions of the best of British farce.

The Japanese Legation was almost directly opposite the British, and with Puyi safe Johnston could relax a little. Not surprisingly, the newspapers had a field day over Puyi's flight to the Japanese Legation. With the knowledge of hindsight, it is easy to see Puyi's actions as those of a man enthused by the Japanese and ready to play his part in their eventual overrun of Manchuria. Johnston remained adamant for the rest of his life that there had never been any grand political conspiracy on the part of the Japanese to support Puyi in 1924.

Puyi celebrated his nineteenth birthday in the Japanese Legation in February 1925. Johnston continued to arrange his diary, and throughout that month organised several engagements for Puyi at the emperor's request. He was shortly to discover that this was simply a deception on Puyi's part. On 24 February Johnston left Puyi with the Japanese at 5.45 pm, planning to return to the Legation the following day at his usual hour, 11 am. He had absolutely no reason to suspect that there was anything untoward. Between seven and eight that same evening, Puyi told his attendants that he was walking over to the British Legation to see Johnston and to attend a dance there. Instead, he left the Japanese Legation and walked to the station with two servants, a trusted official and some Japanese Legation police. They took the first train going to Tianjin, and his wife and his consort followed him the next morning before Johnston arrived at the Japanese Legation.

When Johnston discovered the next day that Puyi had left Beijing, he was hurt and angry. He had been Puyi's companion and confidant for six years and the emperor's treachery was a bitter pill to swallow. What mystified Johnston most was how Puyi had managed to carry off his plan. He knew the youth well – better, perhaps – than anyone else did at that time. Puyi had spent his life in cosseted luxury. He could not tie his own shoelaces, far less organise a train journey. Within hours, Johnston had come to the sad conclusion that the Japanese had made the arrangements for the flight to Tianjin, and that they would now 'use him as a political pawn'. His fears were proved correct when Puyi moved into a hotel and later into a house in the Japanese concession in Tianjin, rather than into the house he already owned there which was in the British concession.

Puyi must have been quite fearful of Johnston's wrath when he phoned his former tutor from Tianjin on the evening of 25 February. Johnston said Puyi begged him to join him there, but his reply was frosty: 'It will be rather a relief to me if I can leave the Emperor's service now, as I don't want to leave Beijing. I have given up the idea of taking him to England, and I think that if the Japanese will have him he had much better go to Japan, and settle down say in or near Kyoto.' The emperor was left in no doubt how hurt and angry Johnston was.

Puyi continued to plead with Johnston to return to his post, and on 9 March Johnston finally submitted to his entreaties and travelled to Tianjin to see him. A treaty port and second only to Shanghai in its cosmopolitan appearance, part of the city was divided into concessions. Each concession, whether it was British, Japanese or French, was a miniature foreign enclave in the midst of a Chinese town. The concessions had rights of extra-territoriality, which meant that the laws of China had no authority in these areas. The Japanese concession was therefore a little piece of Japan set into north-eastern China. The concession in Tianjin was a particularly important one for Japan as it provided her with its main military base in north China and the Japanese area bristled with soldiers.

Johnston stayed there for four days. He remained aloof, refusing Puyi's offer of a room in his own house and electing instead to stay at his own expense in a hotel in Tianjin. They continued to argue about Johnston's resignation. Puyi refused to accept it, and Johnston finally returned to Beijing with his imperial post still, theoretically, in place. Many of the things he saw and heard in Tianjin alarmed Johnston. Puyi was living, rent free, in a comfortable house provided by the Japanese authorities, called Zhang Garden. Although Puyi was no longer bound by the rigid ritual and etiquette which had characterised life in the Forbidden City, he had hardly any more freedom than he had experienced in Beijing, and this concerned Johnston.

Johnston had no time for the people who now surrounded Puyi. A mixture of former courtiers and officials, he felt that their influence in Tianjin was unhealthy for Puyi. He warned Puyi against becoming involved in plots and intrigues, and finally sealed his disapproval of what the emperor had done by telling him that he thought it unwise for him to think any longer of visiting Europe. Puyi was crushed by Johnston's words. For his part, Johnston remained furious with his former charge, and wrote a damning letter to Li Jingmai:

... there is no use disguising the fact that his recent sojourn in the Legation Quarter in Beijing did not increase his prestige among foreigners here .... Unlike the Empress (who charmed everyone), he is lacking in natural dignity and grace of bearing; and such good qualities as he undoubtedly possesses are not such as are readily discernible by strangers. He has also caused me a good deal of trouble and embarrassment by his lack of taste in the matter of dress. In this and other respects he often shows an exasperating obstinacy and unwillingness to listen to advice.

With Puyi's departure from Beijing, Johnston was once more at a crossroads. He had no house and stored his books and belongings retrieved from his home and from his offices in the Forbidden City wherever he could in Beijing. Most importantly, he had no job. For a year or so he had been in receipt of a small pension from the Colonial Office which retained him within the service but did not guarantee him a job. Weihaiwei was now staffed by Consular Officers, so there was no post for him there. He was only 50, and therefore had several years to go until he reached retirement age. A decision about his future had to be reached.

By the autumn of 1925 Johnston had been without a salary for almost a year and he was becoming desperate. Puyi continued to press him to return to his service and it was with some misgiving that he returned to Tianjin. Puyi was delighted to have Johnston back by his side, even though Johnston had warned him that he would leave without notice if the British Government offered him a job at any point. Apart from the frustration of being part of the Imperial Household once more, there was another problem being in Puyi's service. The emperor had hardly any money to pay Johnston and could only offer a salary of $600 a month and accommodation. It was a far cry from the heady days in the Forbidden City when cumshaws were as regular as his salary, but Johnston stayed, bound by his old loyalties to Puyi.

He tried to broaden Puyi's life in the city, introducing him 'to the British consul and the commander of the British garrison'. It is impossible to predict what might have happened to Puyi had Johnston remained in Tianjin for any length of time. The Scot had always had a calming influence on the emperor and usually offered sensible advice. Johnston's belief that Puyi should remain in the city and live as quiet and unassuming life as possible was sound advice at the time, but even he must have despaired of Puyi's future prospects with his dwindling financial situation. In any event, Johnston was not destined to remain in the emperor's service. After only a few weeks in Tianjin – too few to have made an appreciable difference to Puyi's new life – a post was offered to him by the British Government.

Following the Boxer Uprising in 1900, the British Government demanded, and received, an annual payment from China as compensation for the injury caused to British interests. This was an invidious agreement, and one which naturally caused offence to the Chinese Republican Government following the overthrow of the Empire. With an agreement reached at Versailles at the end of the war, it was decided to use the funds which had accrued from the indemnity payments for the mutual benefit of Britain and China. The Boxer Indemnity Committee, chaired by Lord Willingdon, was established to discover the best way to use the funds. These were not inconsiderable. In 1926 they amounted to £500,000 a year. The committee was instructed to visit China to see how to spend the money, and to take with them a British official who spoke Chinese and could act as their secretary. Johnston was the obvious candidate. The Foreign Office recommended his appointment to the committee in the strongest terms.

Johnston had little option but to accept the post, though he was hardly brimming with enthusiasm for it. For one thing, the salary offered was less than that he could have expected in Weihaiwei, being a single fee payment of £1000. Also, the post was a temporary one and after a year Johnston would be in the same position as before. He met the committee in Shanghai on 24 February 1926. The group had set their sights on dispersing the Boxer Indemnity money on a variety of projects concerning education, medicine, river conservation, land reclamation, and road and railway construction. It was Johnston's duty to take notes of their deliberations. Hardly demanding work, but duties which kept him extremely busy. In Shanghai alone, the committee held eight meetings. By the end of their work, they had held more than 50 meetings around the country. By the time these were over, Johnston was thoroughly sick of the entire proceedings.

When the committee's tour of China came to an end, Johnston was sent to Britain to complete his draft of their report. So high was his frustration with the committee and all its works that he decided to make his journey to London via Vancouver and New York. This was the longest possible route back to Britain, and his Pacific crossing gave him the opportunity to write the final report for the committee, in the hope that there would not be much work to do when he reached London.

True to his predictions his visit to London took barely a fortnight. His report was accepted in full by the committee, though he received neither an acknowledgement nor thanks for his work, which was known thereafter as the Willingdon Commission Report. As it was twelve years since his last visit to Britain, he decided to take advantage of the free trip there. After some gentle rambling on the North Yorkshire moors and a visit to the Lake District, he returned to London for the final round of work with the Indemnity Committee. His desire to return to China propelled him to leave London as soon as his work with the committee was over. By October he was once more a free agent, and he promptly booked his passage back to China.

Johnston wanted one final glimpse of Europe before he left, and so planned a visit to Italy, sailing to China from Naples. His itinerary meant that he stayed in London longer than he anticipated, but this gave him the opportunity to see Stewart Lockhart for the first time since 1919. During October, they met for tea and dined together, picking up their friendship as though there had never been any interval at all. There was one other friendship Johnston renewed – very quietly – in London. Eileen Power, the young historian who had been so entranced by Johnston and Cherry Glen when she had visited there in 1921, was now teaching in the city. A reader in Economic History at the London School of Economics, she was making her name as an influential academic. Intelligent and beautiful, Johnston seems to have been as drawn to her as she to him. The meetings with Eileen Power and with the Stewart Lockhart family were all too short, as were the few days he snatched at his beloved Magdalen. As his ship sailed from Naples on 13 December, his 'final fling' in London was a men-only affair at the Overseas League. Old friends, including Stewart Lockhart, were invited to the private room he hired for the evening 'so we can talk as much nonsense and make as much noise as we like'.

His final days in London 'before I leave England probably for ever', were as unpredictable as ever. 'I went to Buckingham Palace yesterday by "command" and found the king very affable and chatty. Mrs Walkinshaw tried to get into the Palace in the fog, but fortunately was ejected just in time. I also went to the C. O. yesterday. They now want to send me back to Weihai to administer the Govt.!' Dumbstruck, Johnston accepted their offer without a second thought. He would have plenty of time to review his decision on the long sea journey back to China.

Chapter 4
1927-1938

JOHNSTON sailed back to China in high spirits. As he was not expected to begin work in Weihaiwei until April 1927, he took advantage of the free time he had to visit Hong Kong. There, he stayed in the considerable splendour of Government House as a guest of his old friend Cecil Clementi. Clementi had been appointed Governor of the colony in 1925, and Johnston – admittedly not the most impartial of judges – declared that 'he makes an excellent Governor'. Johnston spent three enjoyable weeks with Clementi before visiting Puyi in Tianjin. He found the former Imperial Court in a sorry state. Reliant on Japanese support and money, Puyi was viewed as a pariah by the Chinese. When Johnston left him to travel to his 'delectable' Weihaiwei, Puyi was sadder than most to see him leave and Johnston was overwhelmed with presents from him as he departed.

Britain had been trying to return Weihaiwei to China since the end of World War I. An agreement was reached between the two countries, and the date for the handover set for 22 October 1924: the very day that Feng Yuxiang marched on Beijing, overthrew the Government there, and threatened Puyi. Not surprisingly the return of Weihaiwei was postponed. The political situation was no better throughout the next two years, so the territory remained in British hands.

The Weihaiwei to which Johnston returned on 31 March 1927 was but a shadow of the pretty little place he had left eight years earlier. The English school had closed down and many British residents had left the territory. Even Government House looked neglected. The uncertainty which had prevailed for years over Weihaiwei's future had taken its toll and Johnston was unsure what to expect. He knew he would be living in Government House, but for how long was another question.

Despite the run-down appearance of the place, Johnston found some things exactly as he had left them. He reported to Stewart Lockhart: 'I really don't think that any good purpose will be served by a continuance of your efforts and mine to get the Weihaiwei Moon to behave herself. She is just as bad as ever she was. She simply *refuses* to wear her trousers!' Within days Johnston was hoping that rendition would happen later rather than sooner. 'The longer it is postponed, the better I shall be pleased, as it is delightful to be back in the old place and to find the people as friendly as ever.' He was determined to make the most of his days in Weihaiwei. He never quite became accustomed to living in Government House without the Stewart Lockhart family, but he did manage to adopt the conviviality of the former Commissioner with relative ease. After only six weeks he was complaining that the £150 he was given for entertainment had already been spent. His enjoyment was mirrored in the feelings of local residents: 'The Chinese like Mr Johnston very much – it's nice to feel that at last there is somebody at the top of the tree who takes an interest in the place and doesn't want to take something out of it.'

Johnston was quick to realise that if he did not ask for more money for improvements in Weihaiwei as soon as possible, then he would lose any advantage he had. Even so, it took several months to get what he wanted. By the end of the year he had been given permission to build new roads to connect the various parts of the territory. Weihaiwei had had electricity for a few years, but now Johnston had telephone systems installed in parts of the territory as well. Slowly, he was dragging the place into the twentieth century. As the various measures he put into place began to take effect, even the Colonial Office began to take notice of how much he was achieving. One senior official wrote that 'Mr Johnston impresses me as a hardheaded man worthy of a better post'.

Weihaiwei's prosperity brought further improvements in its wake. Johnston introduced motorised buses to the area, offering public transport for the first time to the people of the territory. More roads were built to connect even more villages to Port Edward. The Chinese of Weihaiwei, settled and prosperous, with no threat of war or famine in their villages, naturally supported their enthusiastic Commissioner. Soon Weihaiwei sparkled as it had not done for years, especially when the Treasury, in a fit of uncharacteristic magnanimity, doubled his entertainment allowance. Johnston threw himself into the spirit of that summer: 'I have also been in an aeroplane, and down in a submarine.' Rarely had he been so happy.

In the midst of all this activity he maintained contact with Puyi who continued, despite his perilous financial position, to send Johnston gifts, including a memorial scroll for the Government School. There was one problem, however, 'The Emperor himself wants to come and stay here with me, but I have had to explain reluctantly that I fear H.M.'s Government would not approve.' These requests were written secretly by Puyi and sent to Johnston via an intermediary. Despite so many years in China, his Scottish canniness had not deserted Johnston: 'I am keeping his autograph letters to me: perhaps someday they will postpone my entry into the Workhouse.'

The year 1928 ended particularly pleasantly. First of all, Johnston received his Honorary Degree from the University of Hong Kong – ten years after it had been awarded to him. Then, in October, he wrote to Stewart Lockhart with the news that he had a rather special guest staying with him: 'I have a much more charming person than Mrs Walkinshaw (The Quork) staying with me at present: namely Miss (!!!) Eileen Power, whose distinguished career you may find in *Who's Who*.' The local inhabitants of the territory were accustomed to their Commissioner entertaining guests in Government House, but guests usually came in pairs. Eileen Power was only 40, extremely attractive, and single. She was also without a chaperone. Her visit therefore inevitably became the subject of gossip in Port Edward. She was his guest throughout the festive period, and with some considerable glee Johnston recorded a few of the local ladies' reactions to his female companion:

Had I not been a decayed old man all Weihaiwei would have been ablaze with scandal! One of the few advantages of being far gone in senile decay is that one

is not apt to be the subject of scandal: though Miss Gresham [a local
missionary] ... *asked me in solemn tones if it was true that I had had a niece
staying with me, and when I said she was not a niece but a great friend, she
gave utterance to a prolonged 'oh!' to intimate her intense disapproval.*

Johnston was quite undismayed by the reaction of such ladies; after all,
he argued, 'we had to do something to provide Weihaiwei with some
gossip, and I think we succeeded'.

It was years since Johnston had had any real female companionship.
Now in his fifty-sixth year, he must have been fascinated and flattered
to receive the attentions of such a vivacious, intelligent woman. When
Eileen left for Japan for a conference, she confided to an associate, who
had also stayed in Weihaiwei with Johnston, that he had asked her to
marry him. Despite their obvious attraction for each other, Johnston
was not sure exactly what Eileen's decision was going to be. Whatever it
was, he planned 'to settle down somewhere with my books, and to find
time and opportunity to knock into shape some of the numerous half-
written books I have in hand. If I have no special inducement to live in
England I shall probably settle in a sunnier climes'.

With Eileen gone, at least temporarily, from his life, Johnston could
once more concentrate on the practicalities of rendition. An agreement
between the two countries was signed in April 1930 and 1 October was
agreed as the date of return. As the day of rendition approached,
Johnston was involved in organising the ceremony, and taking care to
find places for all the Government paraphernalia that had accumu-
lated during 30 years of British rule. He asked Stewart Lockhart if he
wanted anything, and the former Commissioner had only one request:
that the woven silk badge of the territory which normally hung in
the Commissioner's office should be kept for him if at all possible.
Depicting the emblem of Weihaiwei, a Mandarin Duck, Johnston
promised to 'take it or send it home'. The framed weaving now hangs in
the Stewart Lockhart Collection in Edinburgh.

The Colonial Office, always keen to impress, ensured that Johnston
would hand over the territory as a knight of the realm. In June 1930

he became Sir Reginald. Typically, Johnston made light of the honour. 'The Quork asked me whether she could now call herself "Lady Walkinshaw" and was livid with rage when I replied with a most emphatic "No".' The Chinese appointed their own Commissioner to take over from Johnston. Called Commander Xu, Johnston was rather amused to discover when they met that he had been part of the inner circle around Feng Yuxiang when he evicted Puyi from the Forbidden City. Despite being on opposite sides of the political fence, the two men appear to have got on famously.

Britain's final few hours in Weihaiwei were filled with ceremonial. At 10.15 on a chilly morning on the first day of October, guests and spectators assembled on the terrace of Government House. Johnston later remarked: 'The weather couldn't have been more unkind, it was blowing a strong westerly gale, very cold, and showers kept falling, the Chinese at once said it was not a good omen.' Fifteen minutes after the guests had assembled, Commander Xu formally stepped on to the pier at Port Edward to be greeted by a 15-gun salute. The pier was lined with a ceremonial guard of 100 British soldiers and sailors. A naval band played in welcome, and the soldiers looked resplendent in their kilts. Xu then made the short drive up to Government House where he was greeted by Johnston. The little territory had put on a splendid show for their new masters. At Government House a parade was organised with bands, a bugler, 100 sailors, and 50 more kilted soldiers. Commander Xu arrived on the terrace to the strains of the British National Anthem being played for the last time in Weihaiwei.

The moment of history finally came at 10.45 am. When Johnston read out extracts from the rendition agreement in Chinese and English, his emotions were running high. As the Chinese flag rose to join that of Britain, the band played the Chinese National Anthem. British battleships fired their guns in salute from the harbour as the Union Jack came down. The massed ranks of soldiers marched off the parade ground. To commemorate the event, Johnston 'was presented with a splendid silver cup' by the Chinese. By now the intense emotion of the day was too much for him. He 'left hurriedly ... nobody had a handshake … and everybody thought he wouldn't turn round and wave a final farewell'. He never did give that final goodbye. Barely an hour after rendition, Johnston sailed from Weihaiwei on board HMS *Sandwich* bound for Shanghai. Weihaiwei once more belonged to China.

Johnston had always hoped that, when he left Weihaiwei, he would have the opportunity to visit Cherry Glen one last time. That wish was never fulfilled. Instead, having sailed to Shanghai he immediately travelled to Britain. He had two pressing reasons to return without delay: Eileen Power had agreed to marry him, and he had decided to apply for the Chair of Chinese at the School of Oriental Studies in London.

He and Eileen announced their engagement in December 1930. They planned to marry quickly, in January 1931, but their engagement was not a success. Johnston changed his mind more than once about a date for the wedding, and gradually Eileen began to have her own second thoughts about their union. In the spring of 1931 he paid scant attention to his fiancée as he travelled up and down the country seeing friends he had not met for years. He was still uncertain as to whether or not he would get the London Chair, and he made no secret of the fact that, were that post to fall through, then he would almost certainly leave Britain. With her own demanding and prestigious career, this was hardly the kind of news Eileen Power wanted to hear. In the summer of 1931 they again postponed the wedding and a year later the engagement was finally dissolved by Eileen. There were no hard feelings on either side and they remained in close contact and to be friends. The only surprise is that Eileen took so long to make her decision.

In March, Johnston was interviewed for, and appointed to, the Chair of Chinese at the University of London's School of Oriental Studies. The School should have realised what they were getting when Johnston, no sooner appointed to the post, informed them that he would need five month's leave of absence to go to China as a member of the Universities' China Delegation.

Johnston left for China in August 1931, arriving in Shanghai six weeks later to study various educational schemes with a view to giving them financial assistance. Apart from his fluent Chinese, Johnston's contribution to the delegation he was with was marginal. In truth, the trip was simply a way to visit Puyi and have his passage paid. Twice he travelled to Tianjin to see him. At the time, rumours were rife that Puyi would be going to Manchuria, and many in the press surmised that Johnston's appearance in China had something to do with this. The press reports were incorrect, but Johnston reluctantly agreed with Puyi that Manchuria could be no worse than Tianjin, although he did have reservations about such a move. Once more, he was entirely correct in his analysis of the situation. Puyi was smuggled out of Tianjin in November 1931, eventually reaching Manchuria early in 1932. There he became a puppet of his Japanese masters.

Johnston finally returned to London at the beginning of 1932 to take up his professorial duties. He was required to teach for up to 14 hours a week and to run a small department. From the start it was a disaster. Johnston could be an inspiring lecturer, but when he was asked to lecture series after series, he was boring and bored. On one occasion he cut short a block of lectures mid-session, on the grounds that he had 'more than exhausted the subject, besides exhausting myself in trying to avoid repetition'. He absented himself when it suited him, ignored all administration and was the despair of the university authorities.

The long academic vacations did, however, give him time to write. In 1925 he had begun a book about his years in the Forbidden City, but it was not until 1932 that he had the opportunity to complete it. *Twilight in the Forbidden City* was published just over a year later. He dedicated the book to Puyi, who had written a brief preface for it when they met in Tianjin the previous year. Although Puyi was now denigrated by the international community as Japan's puppet ruler, Johnston's bonds with him were too strong to relinquish. They continued to correspond, and Puyi's sister, Madame Zheng, and her husband stayed with him in his house at Kew, near London. The family remained there for more than a year, and their first baby was born in his home. When his imperial guests finally left in March 1934 to return to Manchuria, Johnston admitted, 'I shall miss them greatly'. Having the family there made him long to see Puyi again.

His closeness to the Imperial Family caused its problems for Johnston. Chinese students in London loathed his connection with the emperor and his family. Feelings ran sufficiently high for Johnston to decide to curtail his outings to places where he would encounter Chinese students, such as the China Society. It was ludicrous to have a Professor of Chinese who was effectively barred from a range of Chinese venues, but Johnston shrugged off the animosity against him. He had rarely cared about the opinions of the outside world, and was too old to change now, even if he wanted to.

Johnston doubtless felt vindicated in his support of Puyi when *Twilight in the Forbidden City* was published at the beginning of 1934. The book was reviewed kindly and sold better than anything else he had written. Until then, his role in the Forbidden City had been known to a relatively closed circle of China enthusiasts. Now his story reached a mass audience and Johnston became a minor celebrity. Within a few months the book was being published in a fourth edition, was selling equally well in America, and was being translated into Japanese.

Shortly after this, he completed his next, and final, book, *Confucianism in Modern China*. This was an easy volume to write, based as it was on a series of lectures he had delivered at Bristol University. He had a marvellous time during his lecture series – far more so than he ever had at London University. The main reason for this was that the Vice-Chancellor of the University was none other than his old friend Loveday. It was with great pleasure that he could at last repay Loveday's unstinting friendship by giving the lectures.

The success of *Twilight in the Forbidden City* made a large impact on his bank balance and he decided to spend it on acquiring a retreat. Nominally, of course, he still had Cherry Glen, but knew he would never see it again. Before he left China he had allowed it to be used by students from the British Legation, but banditry was increasingly prevalent in the Western Hills and the place was eventually abandoned. Therefore, in July 1934, he set off for the Scottish Highlands to find a new abode. Travelling to the western county of Argyll, he found 'an island that has been offered to me at a low price ... on Loch Craignish

– a sea loch between Ardrishaig and Oban'. Johnston immediately fell in love with the property. The main island was low and flat. Called Eilean Righ – the Island of the King – it nestled only a few hundred yards from a rocky shore. The island was about two miles long, with four and a half miles of shoreline – not too big to get lost in, but small enough to get to know well. There were other advantages. 'The house is only a simple little farmhouse, but there is a very large barn which can easily be converted into a spacious library'.

By September Johnston had purchased the Eilean Righ estate for £1600 and was living there. He even had headed notepaper printed and wrote proudly to Stewart Lockhart about his little Highland estate. 'I am the possessor of three islands, of which this is the largest and the one with the house. It is only a humble farm-house but I am having the farm-steading, which adjoins it, converted into part of the house and I shall then have a large room – as large as a full-sized billiard room – for a library.' It could not have been more perfect.

Johnston spent Christmas and New Year on his island. As ever, his first concern was his library. Pride of place was given to the Chinese books Puyi had presented to him during his years in the Forbidden City. Some of these were particularly important because 'they were printed in the imperial Palace for the use of the imperial family and house-hold, and have never been obtainable in the book-market'. But Johnston had other volumes which he lovingly set out on the shelves. A Chinese encyclopaedia in 1734 volumes decorated one area in the room. Then there were his complete collection of Buddhist scriptures in 1500 volumes, his collection of mountain chronicles in 250 volumes, and his compendium of Chinese literature in 1200 volumes. Under-standably, it did not take long to fill the large room. With many of his books in place, Johnston felt that Eilean Righ was truly his 'home', and he was indeed loathe to leave the island to return to London in January.

In April 1935 one of his guests was a Mrs Elizabeth Sparshott, who was making her first visit to the island in the company of her daughter, Jessica. Johnston mentioned to Stewart Lockhart that he was playing host to them, describing Mrs Sparshott as a widow. This was the first, but not the last, lie he was to tell for the woman who was to be the final love of his life. Elizabeth Sparshott was a Londoner, born in 1893. During World War I she had married Tom Sparshott and, in 1918, her only daughter was born. She first met Johnston in 1934, following the publication of *Twilight in the Forbidden City,* when she wrote to him at the University 'asking to meet the author'. Johnston agreed to her request, liked the tall, handsome, and very smartly dressed woman he met, and gradually they got to know one another. By all accounts she was a shy, quiet woman and he fell deeply in love with her. Elizabeth reciprocated his love, even though she was still married to Tom Sparshott. The marriage had certainly broken down long before she met Johnston, but there was still an enormous stigma attached to extra-marital affairs in the 1930s, hence Johnston's description of her as a widow.

Johnston left Eilean Righ at the end of July to pay a visit to Puyi. Now Emperor of Manchukuo, as the Japanese called Manchuria, Puyi was determined to show his former tutor what a good decision he had made in moving there. Changchun had been declared the new capital of the country following the Japanese invasion. Johnston had a magnificent time, even though the Court of the Emperor of Manchukuo had fewer of the trappings and magnificence of his previous one in the Forbidden City. Changchun, for a start, had none of the cosmopolitan atmosphere of Tianjin, far less Beijing. It was little more than a grand railway junction, situated at the point where all the railways which crossed the country met. It was a small town, with no distinctive architecture, and Puyi's own home was the former Salt Tax Palace in the city. Built in brick by the Russians some years before, it had its own compound and was surrounded by high walls. Unless he was visiting his office (in which case he was accompanied by Japanese guards), or undertaking some official duty, he did not leave the house. Once more he was a prisoner, this time in a police state. Still, Puyi swaggered about dressed in European clothes bedecked with medals, like some tin-pot general. It was a sad life, and Johnston's presence must have been a welcome respite from his usual existence. Puyi certainly continued to have a deep affection for his former tutor. But when Puyi repeatedly asked him to stay, Johnston refused; the love of Elizabeth Sparshott was too strong to ignore. After four months with Puyi, he bade his farewells. It was the last time he was to see his little emperor.

The summer of 1936 was once more spent on Eilean Righ. Elizabeth Sparshott stayed for part of the time, and together they improved and enlarged parts of the house, and even gave some of the rooms names; the Emperor Room, the Weihaiwei Room, and the Bamboo Room. With Cherry Glen in mind they had a little temple built, and planted hundreds of irises, Johnston's favourite flower, in the grounds. He was by now quite infatuated with Elizabeth, and was living with her as though they were a married couple. She declared that she 'did love Rex so truly – to the best and utmost of my capacity'. Some people found her a pleasant person; other friends of Johnston's were less flattering.

Many of those who knew and admired Johnston most were the ones who damned Elizabeth Sparshott in the strongest terms. Eileen Power, who knew Elizabeth and was generally generous where Johnston was concerned, described her as 'an unsophisticated creature'. The Stewart Lockhart family did not like her at all. Mary Stewart Lockhart believed her to be an unsavoury character, and when the family finally discovered that she was a married woman, their outrage was intense. Johnston told few people that Elizabeth Sparshott was going to seek a divorce from her husband, but he did tell Stewart Lockhart. Sir James made his disapproval known in no uncertain terms. At that time, divorce carried in its wake enormous scandal, and the fact that Johnston was going to be named as the guilty party in court did nothing to lessen Stewart Lockhart's dismay. For the first time in their lives, they fell out badly with one another. Stewart Lockhart would have nothing to do with Elizabeth. Things reached a head when Johnston took her to Sir James' house in London in the winter of 1936 and Stewart Lockhart would not greet her. He died a few months later, in February 1937, without healing the rift with Johnston.

In the same year, having lived together for almost a year 'to make sure we were suited', Johnston and Elizabeth decided to marry. Johnston was cited as the co-respondent in her divorce papers and they expected to hold a private wedding ceremony in October 1938, on or about his sixty-fourth birthday. Christmas Day of 1937 was spent quietly, with just Johnston, Elizabeth and her daughter Jessica on their peaceful little island. However, the following day Johnston was sick and, uncharacteristically for him, spent the whole day in bed. He continued to be ill during the next few days, and for the rest of January he spent much of his time in bed, alone, writing letters to old friends such as Eileen Power, but never intimating to any of them that he was less than hale and hearty. Finally, in early February, he visited his doctor in Edinburgh. The news was not overly bad, but an operation to remove a kidney stone was required. Elizabeth came up from London to see him in the nursing home in Edinburgh and stayed with him while the operation was performed.

On 20 February 1938 Johnston had his operation. In many ways it was a success. The stone was removed, but the surgeon then discovered that one of Johnston's kidneys had failed and that poison was already seeping through his system. Despite this knowledge, Elizabeth decided to go back to London, where she sat through a few of Eileen Power's lectures. Only at the beginning of March, when Johnston's condition began to deteriorate, did Elizabeth return to Edinburgh. She sat at his bedside for the final two days, watching as Johnston died on 6 March.

When he had written to his lawyer three weeks earlier, Johnston rewrote his will and made known his wishes for a funeral. At his request, the ceremony was private. He was cremated at Warriston Crematorium, just opposite the cemetery where his parents were buried. The simple ceremony, without any religious service, was held two days after he died, with only Elizabeth Sparshott and his lawyer, Euan Robertson, in attendance. Deliberately held before even an obituary notice could be filed, it ensured that Johnston departed from this earth as was his wish, with as little fuss as possible. Carrying his ashes, Euan Robertson and Elizabeth Sparshott then made the long journey back to Eilean Righ. There, on 10 March, his ashes were scattered across the land he loved.

It was a solemn occasion, with a lone piper playing a final lament.

His wishes had been carried out, but Johnston would doubtless have roared with laughter – and blamed Mrs Walkinshaw – for the fiasco which took place. 'A piper was there from Craignish .... The wind was very strong and the ashes blew back into the piper's face. However later he assured a neighbour that for the same fee he wouldn't have minded a second mouthful!' Even in death, Johnston could make the predictable unpredictable.

Johnston was at least at peace, his remains (in part) scattered over his beloved estate. The uproar which followed his death was, however, to shatter any illusions that his memory might be left in similar peace. In his final letter to the lawyers, he had instructed that certain named people should be informed of his death by letter. He asked only that Elizabeth and his cousin Douglas should be notified by telegram. His former fiancée, Eileen Power, and old friends, were to receive the news via a letter from his lawyers. In several instances the letters arrived after the first obituary notices appeared. Eileen Power discovered that Johnston had died when she opened *The Times* newspaper and saw his obituary. She was 'shocked and grieved beyond measure'.

Other friends were equally stunned by the news. Mary Stewart Lockhart, who had bestowed her adoration on him since her child-hood, received the news in the same unexpected manner that Eileen Power had. Loveday and Clementi were more fortunate, receiving the lawyer's letter before they read any obituaries. Loveday's reaction was typical of a man who had seen Johnston seldom since their days together at Magdalen, but who had maintained a friendship with him nevertheless. He wrote that Johnston's death 'is a sad loss to scholarship and a jagged wound to those who loved him'.

The events surrounding his will were to cause further anxiety. Johnston willed 'all my Loch Craignish properties to the National Trust for Scotland, with the proviso that ... Mrs Sparshott should be allowed to occupy the house and have custody of all my moveable property there for the rest of her life or for so long as she wished to make use of them'. Elizabeth Sparshott was not short of money, and had her own independent means, so it was reasonable for Johnston to believe that she would carry out his stated wishes to the letter. The first, predictable, objections to the will came from Johnston's sister, Noney, who immediately tried, unsuccessfully, to contest it. Despite Johnston's wishes, Elizabeth never did give his islands or their contents to the National Trust. On the very day that he died she penned a letter to his lawyers requesting that they urgently negotiate with the National Trust to 'see the islands and once and for all refuse them'. And although the National Trust made it clear straight away that 'they might be prepared to take over the islands', she decided to sell them and keep the proceeds for herself. As quickly as she could – some would say with unseemly haste – she realised all the assets Johnston had left her. She even asked the lawyers to try and get some money for Cherry Glen. It was with regret that she discovered that the place had been looted in 1937 and fell into ruin at the hands of bandits shortly after.

Elizabeth Sparshott then carried out her final, most disastrous, act. Johnston had asked her 'to write a biography of him and gave [her] a mass of material'. Over the years he had not only kept all his notes of his travels, but also all his manuscripts, finished and unfinished, as well as a huge numbers of letters, a correspondence which presented a unique picture of 40 critical years in the history of China. Elizabeth decided she would not write his story. One might have expected her to at least try to accord with Johnston's wish by either keeping all the papers together for a future biographer to use under her direction, or to gift them, as she did the books, to some academic institution or library. Instead, she destroyed them all.

Within five months of Johnston's death, his house had been emptied of its contents, the islands had been sold, and his furniture dispersed through salesrooms. After death duties and taxes had been paid, Elizabeth Sparshott was left with £5000. She kept a few mementoes. The sable cloak was retained in its glass case, and she also kept all the gifts from Puyi. With a delicious irony, she gave his precious library to the School of Oriental Studies, the one academic establishment he had hated. By the summer of 1938, Elizabeth Sparshott had distributed Johnston's belongings to the four winds.

During his life, Johnston had done everything in his power to obliterate the existence of his family from his memory. On his death, Elizabeth did her best to ensure that every other ounce of his personal life was similarly eradicated. It was as though she did not want to share Johnston with anyone else. She almost achieved her aim. What she could not have predicted, however, was that the actions of others would overcome her unfortunate intentions. This process began, ironically, with Puyi. The feckless young man who had never been in control of his own destiny was to be the first to resurrect his memory. In 1945 Russia invaded Manchuria and defeated the Japanese. Puyi spent just over four years as their prisoner before being handed back to China in 1950. After nine years in a Chinese prison, he was encouraged, as part of the rehabilitation process, to write his own story. Despite a lengthy 'remoulding' under Mao's regime in China, his resulting auto-biography was to give Johnston an existence once more.

Puyi was the first person to write about Johnston at length, but his memory was not forgotten by other friends. Loveday kept all the letters that Johnston sent to him, from the heady days as students to his final months on Eilean Righ. Today, they are still lovingly preserved by Loveday's family. Despite their final, acrimonious parting, Stewart Lockhart never forgot his friend and colleague. Johnston wrote more than 600 letters to him and they too were lovingly preserved by Mary Stewart Lockhart who eventually gifted them to her father's former school in Edinburgh. These, and the British Government's habit of preserving a high percentage of official papers, ensured that Johnston the friend, the scholar, tutor and government officer, would live on.

Had his estate not been so badly treated, and had we, today, been able to read through Johnston's own papers, the story of his life might have been told in a different way. Gaps might have been filled, incidents related in more detail. However, the essential picture of Johnston would have certainly remained the same. Reginald Johnston was a strange, difficult and eccentric man. He was both clever and foolish, amusing and annoying, liberal and biased. But more than anything else, he was predictably unpredictable. To the very end, he was an enigma.

Further Reading

Airlie, Shiona M: *Thistle And Bamboo: The Life And Times Of Sir James Stewart Lockhart* (Hong Kong, Oxford University Press 1989).

Battye, Evelyn: 'Picnic Summer In Wei-hai-wei', in *Country Life* (22 May 1986), pp 1464-1466.

Behr, Edward: *The Last Emperor* (London, Futura 1987).

Berg, Maxine: *A Woman In History: Eileen Power 1889-1940* (Cambridge, Cambridge University Press 1996).

Bickers, Robert A: '"Coolie Work": Sir Reginald Johnston at the School of Oriental Studies, 1931-1937', in *Journal of the Royal Asiatic Society*, Third Series, volume 5, part 3 (November 1995).

Fairbank, John King: *The Great Chinese Revolution: 1800-1985* (New York, Harper and Row 1986).

Johnston, Reginald F: *Account Of A Journey In Shantung From Weihaiwei To The Tomb Of Confucius* (Weihaiwei 1904).

Johnston, Reginald F (as Lin Shaoyang): *A Chinese Appeal Concerning Christian Missions* (London, Watts and Company 1911).

Johnston, Reginald F: *Buddhist China* (London, John Murray 1913).

Johnston, Reginald F: *Confucianism And Modern China: The Lewis Fry Memorial Lectures 1933-4* (London, Victor Gollancz Limited 1934).

Johnston, Reginald F: *From Peking To Mandalay: A Journey from North China to Burma through Tibetan Ssuch'uan and Yunnan* (London, John Murray 1908).

Johnston, Reginald F: *Letters To A Missionary* (London, Watts and Company 1918).

Johnston, Reginald F: *Lion And Dragon In Northern China* (London, John Murray 1910). (Reprinted Hong Kong, Oxford University Press 1986).

Johnston, Reginald F: *Remarks On The Province Of Shantung* (Hong Kong, Noronha and Company 1904).

Johnston, Reginald F (as Theodoric): *The Last Days Of Theodoric The Ostrogoth And Other Verses* (London, Simpkin, Marshall and Co. 1904).

Johnston, Reginald F: *Twilight in the Forbidden City* (London, Victor Gollancz Ltd 1934). (Reprinted Hong Kong, Oxford University Press 1983).

Loveday, Thomas (transcribed by Mrs Sarah Markham): *Memories Of Oxford In 1894. Reminiscences of Thomas Loveday* (Magdalen College Record, Oxford 1983).

Loveday, Thomas (transcribed by Mrs Sarah Markham): *Memories Of Magdalen And Oxford. Reminiscences of Thomas Loveday* (Magdalen College Record, Oxford 1984).

Pu Yi: *From Emperor To Citizen: The Autobiography Of Aisin-Gioro Pu Yi*, translated and with an introduction by W J F Jenner (Oxford, Oxford University Press 1987).

Wood, Francis: *No Dogs And Not Many Chinese; Treaty Port Life In China 1843-1943* (London, John Murray 1998).
America 24, 94

Index